TEACHING IN ENGLAND POST-1988

Accounts of change in education tend to focus on capturing how policy is developed at a system level. *Teaching in England Post-1988* is important because it examines a 30-year period of unprecedented change in English schools through in-depth interviews which capture the lived experiences of some of the teachers who survived it. This enables it to offer a detailed, longitudinal perspective that remains all too rare, and new insights into how and why teachers maintain their commitment to teaching and schools in the face of increasing pressures and demands. As a result, it should be read carefully by everyone interested in the future of schools and of education more widely.

—Michael Jopling, Professor of Education, University of Brighton

Joan Woodhouse has applied her considerable experience as both a teacher and a teacher educator to bring to our attention the previously under-researched phenomenon of teacher retention. While other researchers and the mass media have focussed on the issue of early leavers, Woodhouse details the creativity and tenacity of those who have responded to ever-shifting policies which have increased prescription and proscription, heralded the erosion of teachers' autonomy and creativity, imposed longer working hours and increased workload, and facilitated changes in the culture of schooling and the nature of teaching. The essential question – Why have these career-long teachers remained in the profession, when so many of their peers quit? – is addressed through enlightening and original accounts which offer deeper understanding of how this generation of teachers navigated the changes and sustained their commitment to teaching. 'Vocation', 'wisdom' and 'agency' are shown to be their essential characteristics, which provides a much-needed antidote to the doom and gloom image of teachers as burnt-out automatons often promulgated in public discourse.

Career teachers should enjoy reading this well-researched and well-written text in the knowledge that they are not alone in their dedication. Anyone considering teaching as a profession will find much to comfort them, and to arm them for the challenges they will face. Policy-makers, who rarely seem informed by research which doesn't fit their preconceptions, would particularly benefit from understanding the damage they have wrought and identifying potential remedial strategies by reading about the real experiences of dedicated professionals.

—Ralph Leighton, Former Principal Lecturer and Secondary
PGCE Programme Director, Canterbury Christ Church University

This book could not be more timely: with teachers leaving the profession in droves, and teacher recruitment at an all-time low, it is vital that we learn more about the experiences of those who have remained in the profession for some time. Dr Woodhouse is ideally placed to give this account, based on her long experience working with teachers, and as a former teacher herself. It will be useful to post grad and PGCE students and, from both theoretical and practical perspectives, represents a valuable contribution to the literature.

—Professor Jacqueline Baxter, Professor of Public Leadership and Management, The Open University

Joan Woodhouse has created a fascinating and innovative history of education from 1988 through the eyes of long-serving teachers whose vision and wisdom has enabled them to have marathon careers in times when many teachers have left the profession. Her own wisdom and vision – which I've known for years since we taught together in the 1980s – make this a provocative and vital read for all who care about teaching and teacher supply.

—Lat Blaylock, Editor, RE Today magazine, National RE adviser, NATRE

This book is exactly what is needed currently. The teacher recruitment and retention crisis, the meltdown in the initial teacher education 'space' wrought by the ideologically motivated 'market review', and the well-documented impact of the pandemic on teachers' well-being, welfare and willingness to remain in the profession, all contribute to its necessity. Insufficient qualitative research has been undertaken on why teachers leave. What exists are statistics and trends which show the outcomes, not the reasons. Even less qualitative research has been undertaken on why teachers stay, up to this point. Politicians tend not to ask; system leaders are more concerned about performance and outcomes, and armchair analysts assume they have an authentic answer to everything. Joan's approach here builds on her years as a successful classroom teacher, teacher trainer and educational researcher. She builds positive and mutually respectful relationships with peers and those she's teaching. Few others could successfully administer a research tool such as this because of its dependence on professional, collaborative relationships. Consequently, the findings are genuinely authentic, giving this book a degree of validity and reliability, in a sector dominated by external perceptions of truth.

—Dr Simon Hughes FRSA, Freelance Educational Adviser, former Her Majesty's Inspector and former diocesan Director of Education

TEACHING IN ENGLAND POST-1988: REFLECTIONS AND CAREER HISTORIES

BY

JOAN WOODHOUSE
University of Leicester, UK

United Kingdom – North America – Japan – India
Malaysia – China

Emerald Publishing Limited
Emerald Publishing, Floor 5, Northspring, 21-23 Wellington Street, Leeds LS1 4DL

First edition 2023

Reprints and permissions service
Contact: www.copyright.com

British Library Cataloguing in Publication Data
A catalogue record for this book is available from the British Library

ISBN: 978-1-80382-510-6 (Print)
ISBN: 978-1-80382-509-0 (Online)
ISBN: 978-1-80382-511-3 (Epub)

Printed and bound by CPI Group (UK) Ltd, Croydon, CR0 4YY

INVESTOR IN PEOPLE

In memory of my father, Francis Joseph Smith (1927–2022)

CONTENTS

LIST OF ABBREVIATIONS

'A' level	Advanced level
Cert. Ed.	Certificate of Education
CSE	Certificate of Secondary Education
CPD	Continuing Professional Development
CTCs	City Technology Colleges
CV	Curriculum Vitae
DfE	Department for Education
EAL	English as an Additional Language
ERA	Education Reform Act
ETI	Education and Training Inspectorate
FGM	Female Genital Mutilation
GCSE	General Certificate of Secondary Education
GERM	Global Education Reform Movement
GM	Grant Maintained
HMI	Her/His Majesty's Inspectors or Inspectorate
ICT	Information and Communications Technology
IPA	Interpretative Phenomenological Analysis
ITT	Initial Teacher Training
LEA	Local Education Authority
LGBT	Lesbian, Gay, Bisexual and Transgender
LMS	Local Management of Schools
MAT	Multi Academy Trust
NQT	Newly Qualified Teacher
Ofsted	The Office for Standards in Education, Children's Services and Skills
'O' level	Ordinary Level
PGCE	Postgraduate/Professional Certificate of Education
PISA	Programme for International Student Assessment

RI	Registered Inspector
SATs	Standard Assessment Tests
SEN	Special Educational Needs
SENCo	Special Educational Needs Co-ordinator
SLT	Senior Leadership Team
SPAG	Spelling and Grammar
TA	Teaching Assistant
UK	United Kingdom
USA	United States of America

ACKNOWLEDGEMENTS

I would like to express my sincere thanks to the nine career-long teachers who gave generously of their time to be interviewed for this project, and to the Universities of Nottingham and Leicester for funding the study. I am indebted to my friends and colleagues for their important contributions to the work, in particular to my co-researchers Carmen Mohamed, Phil Wood and Pete Sorensen, our critical friends Howard Stevenson and Djihad Drari, and research assistant Maria Scalise. I am very grateful, too, to Jacqueline Baxter and Gowan Dawson for comments on a first draft, and to my colleagues in the University of Leicester School of Education for their kind consideration in allowing me some space and time for writing. Finally, heartfelt thanks to my husband, John, for ongoing support and feedback, hot dinners and encouragement at all stages.

Chapter 1

TEACHING IN AN ERA OF REFORM: POLICY SHIFT SINCE 1988 IN ENGLISH STATE EDUCATION

INTRODUCTION

This book offers important new insights into career-long teachers' experiences of teaching in England since the Education Reform Act (ERA) (1988). In particular, it offers new understandings of what sustains their longevity in the profession. I draw in the book on data from in-depth, career-history interviews with teachers who had been teaching in the English state sector since the 1970s or 1980s. I discuss (i) the teachers' perceptions of the impact of policy shift on their daily work over a 30-year period (1988–2018), and (ii) the factors the teachers identified as pivotal in enabling them to stay in the profession career-long, when so many of their peers had left before retirement age.[1] (See Table 1 for attrition rates of successive cohorts of teachers.)

These career-long teachers were uniquely placed to offer authentic perspectives on how the succession of changes since 1988 had impacted their work, and on how and why they had been able to remain committed to teaching long term, despite the changing policy landscape. As the participants in the study were nearing the end of their working lives, the timing of the interviews, which took place 30 years after the ERA, was critical. It was a key point at which to harness the perceptions of a group whose seasoned and longitudinal perspective might otherwise have been lost forever. Capturing participants' reflections on 30 years of policy shift, this book also offers a nuanced understanding of the factors that have sustained these teachers career-long in the teaching profession. The teachers' perceptions might usefully inform policymakers and educational leaders concerned with issues of teacher recruitment, retention and attrition. Their reflections also offer valuable insights to individuals considering a career in teaching.

Table 1. Attrition Rate After Number of Years of Service.

Years' Service	6	7	8	9	10	11	12	13	14	15	16	17	18	19	20	21	22	23	24	25
Year Qualified																				
1996	31.9	33.5	36.0	37.6	40.4	41.8	42.6	44.3	42.3	43.2	44.1	45.2	46.3	48.2	50.0	52.2	54.2	55.7	56.7	58.4
1997	31.3	33.4	35.3	38.2	39.6	40.8	42.4	41.0	41.9	42.7	43.7	45.2	47.1	49.0	50.9	52.8	54.5	55.7	57.4	
1998	30.6	32.5	35.6	37.0	38.2	39.8	38.2	39.3	40.3	41.8	43.5	45.3	47.3	49.6	51.4	52.9	54.0	55.9		
1999	30.1	33.4	35.0	36.3	38.3	36.7	38.2	39.4	40.6	42.1	43.8	45.8	47.7	49.5	51.1	52.4	54.2			
2000	31.3	33.3	34.4	36.4	35.1	36.6	37.5	39.2	40.8	42.9	44.8	46.6	48.2	49.9	51.2	52.7				
2001	31.6	32.7	34.5	33.3	34.8	35.9	37.8	39.4	41.3	43.5	45.4	47.3	48.8	49.9	51.3					
2002	30.3	32.4	31.5	33.2	34.6	36.2	38.1	40.1	42.0	44.4	46.2	47.9	49.3	50.9						
2003	30.5	29.9	31.6	33.6	35.3	37.4	39.8	41.9	44.4	46.3	48.2	49.4	51.0							
2004	28.1	30.3	32.3	34.3	36.3	38.5	40.9	43.0	45.2	46.8	47.9	49.7								
2005	28.3	30.4	32.5	34.8	37.4	39.5	42.0	43.9	45.8	47.0	48.6									
2006	28.0	30.6	32.9	35.4	37.9	40.1	42.0	44.0	45.2	47.0										
2007	28.0	30.5	33.5	36.0	38.4	40.7	42.7	43.8	45.3											
2008	27.9	30.8	33.4	35.9	37.9	39.8	41.2	43.1												
2009	29.3	31.8	34.7	36.7	38.8	40.0	41.7													
2010	32.4	34.9	37.3	39.5	40.8	42.6														
2011	33.3	35.3	37.5	38.5	40.3															
2012	33.8	36.0	37.2	38.7																
2013	34.6	35.5	37.4																	
2014	34.1	35.7																		
2015	33.2																			

Data derived from DfE Teaching Workforce Statistics, retrieved from https://www.education.gov.uk.

The aim of the study was to consider the career-long teacher in relation to the changing situation in English state education post-1988. The participants in the study were interviewed during the academic year 2017–2018. They had spent their careers teaching in an era in which there has been an unprecedented pace and rate of policy shift. (See Table 2 for a brief timeline of some key policy shifts referred to by interviewees during our discussions. For a more detailed, chronological list of reports, acts and papers from 1988 to 2018, see Gillard, 2018.) The career-long teachers' insights are critical to understanding this era of reform from the perspective of an under-researched group of educators – those who have experienced and implemented the changes. Their stories reflect how the imposed changes from 1988 onwards were received by already serving teachers, who saw their work as an important, professional role in educating young people. This perception of their role, as I discuss later in the book, was an important factor in their ability to remain committed to teaching.

During the era on which the book focusses, English education witnessed 'a paradigm shift' (Fisher, 2008, p. 255), towards much greater political control and centralisation of education. This paradigm shift was rooted in a significant change in the philosophy underpinning educational provision. This change became apparent in the move from a social to a market-led model, consistent with the free-market ideology that characterised the United States of America (USA) at the time. Successive United Kingdom (UK) governments[2] intensified central, political control of state education. Over time, state education was taken 'further and further away from liberal values, local control of administration and professional input into curricula, teaching methods and examinations' (Fisher, 2008, p. 255).

As a succession of reforms impacted on English state schooling from 1988 onwards, the teachers in this study recalled that they initially experienced anxiety and a sense of loss of control over their own work. Disoriented by the new discourses of performativity, marketisation and competition, they had, arguably, little option but to adapt, or quit. Whilst many of their peers chose to quit (see Hallahan, 2023; see also Table 1), as teachers who had remained in the profession, participants spoke of the ways in which they adapted, shedding light on how the 1988 ERA and subsequent legislation framed their daily work choices. Their stories are testament to the teachers' capacity to reassert control over their work and to use their knowledge, expertise and experience to ensure policy was translated into practice in ways that suited their schools, their contexts and their pupils.

The original insights offered by the study build on a body of research over the last 30 years in which consideration has been given, for example, to

Table 2. Brief Timeline of Key Policy Shifts in English Education.

Dates	Policy	Notes
July 1988	ERA	The basis for a number of subsequent changes, including:
		Basic curriculum to be taught in all maintained schools, comprising National Curriculum and Religious Education (RE): (i) National Curriculum Attainment targets (ATs) set out in National Curriculum, identifying knowledge, skills and understanding pupils are expected to have by the end of each key stage. Pupils assessed against ATs to ascertain progress. National Standard Assessment Tests (SATs) introduced at the end of key stages 1–3 to measure student progress and school performance. Key stages are defined as: • key stage 1: ages 5–7 years (year groups 1–2) • key stage 2: ages 8–11 years (year groups 3–6) • key stage 3: ages 12–14 years (year groups 7–9) • key stage 4: ages 15–16 years (year groups 10–11) (ii) New rules on RE • Schools required to provide a daily act of broadly Christian collective worship. • Local Education Authorities (LEAs) required to set up a standing advisory council on religious education (SACRE), comprising representatives of religious groups, Church of England teachers and LEA. • RE syllabuses to reflect Christian traditions and take into account other main religions.
		Local management of schools (LMS) Pre-1988, schools had control of 'capitation', for expenditure on books and resources. Other financial matters, including staffing and buildings, were the responsibility of the LEA. The 1988 ERA gave school governors control of the majority of the budget, under LMS. School budgets were allocated based on the number and ages of the pupils in the school, plus the number of children with Special Educational Needs (SEN).
		Hiring and dismissal of staff transferred from LEA to school governing bodies.
		Grant maintained (GM) schools GM schools were to be independent of LEAs, with funding from central government, deducted from the LEA budget. Decisions about which schools should seek GM status were based on parental ballots.
		Open enrolment Introducing parental choice in selection of school. Schools' SATs and GCSE results published in 'league tables' to enable parents to choose a suitable school
September 1989	National Curriculum	Roll out starts in maintained schools in England and Wales

(Continued)

Table 2. (*Continued*)

Dates	Policy	Notes
1991	SATs start	The first key stage 1 tests conducted in summer term. Rolled out to subsequent cohorts in following years
March 1992	Education (Schools) Act	Provided for the creation of a new system of school inspection in England and Wales: Ofsted introduced
April 1992	Department for Education established	The Department for Education and Science renamed Department for Education (DfE)
September 1992	HMI ceases to exist	Replaced by Ofsted
1996	National Numeracy Strategy	Strategy outlined expected teaching in primary school Mathematics, covering all years from reception to year 6
1997	National Literacy Strategy	Intended to raise standards in English primary schools, prescriptive guidance on teaching literacy
1997	The Education Act	Reinforcing the 1988 ERA, schools were required to ensure state schools provided children with a curriculum that: • was broad and balanced • promoted spiritual, moral, cultural, mental and physical development • prepared children for adult life • included RE and sex education
September 2002	First, sponsored academies open in England	Academies are state-funded, independent, non-selective schools that run outside of the control of LEAs. The sponsoring body of each academy was required to set up a charitable trust and sign a contract with the DfE. At this stage, most academies were pre-existing schools that converted to academy status having failed Ofsted inspections. Governors appoint staff, set pay and conditions and decide policies
2004	The Children Act	The 'Every Child Matters' policy came into being. Multi-agency approach to supporting children up to age 19. Functions of education and children's social services combined. The term 'LEA' becomes obsolete (although it continued to appear in legislation)
2008	Key Stage 3 SATs abolished	Key stages 1 and 2 SATs retained
2010	The Academies Act	Made it possible for all maintained schools to convert, or be forced, to become academies. Schools graded 'outstanding' by Ofsted are pre-approved. Academies continue to be state funded but enjoy increased autonomy in decisions about curriculum and teachers' pay and conditions
September 2014	National Curriculum levels of attainment removed	

Source: Adapted from Gillard (2018) and Watson (2001).

teacher resilience (Day & Gu, 2014; Day & Hong, 2016), teacher profession-alism as enacted, and as defined in the government's professional standards (see Evans, 2011), and teacher professionalism in relation to accountability and trust (including, e.g., Evans, 2011; Ozga, 1995; Ozga, Baxter, Clarke, & Lawn, 2013; Six, 2021). The study on which this book reports adds a new dimension to our understanding of teachers' experiences in the context of English state education post-1988. It presents a picture of a group of teach-ers who adapted to change in ways that were neither actively resistant nor passively compliant. It provides accounts of the ways in which, over time, the teachers took control of their work to suit the context in which they worked and the children and communities they served.

I begin by discussing, in this introductory chapter, how the ERA (1988), and the policy shifts that ensued thereafter, affected the school sector in Eng-land in the 30 years that followed. (See Table 2 for a brief timeline of the pol-icy shifts to which the teachers in this study refer.) I consider how the change of inspection regime from Her Majesty's Inspectorate (HMI) to the Office for Standards in Education, Children's Services and Skills (Ofsted) altered the culture and practices of inspection. Finally, I provide a brief overview of the chapters that follow.

THE ERA (1988) AND AFTER

The ERA (1988) marks the start of a period of over 30 years during which there has been an 'epidemic of reform' (Ball, 2003, p. 215) in English educa-tion. Prior to this period, the legacy of the Education Act of 1944 had been a more liberal system, in which LEAs were empowered to effect change, and government did not intervene (Fisher, 2008).

The ERA (1988) was to some extent the outcome of a growing, cross-party concern that, compared with other countries, state schools were under-performing, and young people were not being properly prepared for work and society. Teachers and educational administrators were suspected of 'run-ning the system in their own interests and obscuring the results from public accountability' (Fisher, 2008, p. 257). This suspicion is apparent, for example, in some of the comments made by Labour Prime Minister James Callaghan in his Ruskin College speech (1976):

> [S]ome people would wish that the subject matter and purpose of education should not have public attention focused on it [...] We all know those who claim to defend standards but who in reality are simply seeking to defend old privileges and inequalities [...]

> *To the teachers I would say that you must satisfy the parents and industry that what you are doing meets their requirements and the needs of our children [...] [S]ome of the fields that [...] need study because they cause concern [...] are the methods and aims of informal instruction [and] the strong case for the so-called 'core curriculum' [...]; next, what is the proper way of monitoring the use of resources in order to maintain a proper national standard of performance [...]; [and] the role of the inspectorate in relation to national standards. (Callaghan, 1976)*

Callaghan's concerns were to an extent echoed in Margaret Thatcher's Conservative Party manifesto of 1987 (cited by Gillard, 2018), which promised four major reforms in education:

- a national core curriculum;

- governing bodies and head teachers of all secondary schools and many primary schools to be given control over their own budgets;

- increased parental choice; and

- state schools to be allowed to opt out of LEA control.

Based squarely on the conservative manifesto, the ERA (1988) introduced a number of significant changes. The salient features of the ERA (1988) included:

(i) *A National Curriculum,* defining curriculum content to be taught. The National Curriculum was introduced in 1989 and rolled out over a number of years across primary and secondary schools. National Curriculum focussed primarily on core subjects such as mathematics, science and English, deemed by policymakers to provide better value for money and to equip young people more suitably for employment (McGuire, 2022). Curriculum and assessment were to be organised around key stages, that is, blocks of years at the end of which children would be formally assessed, using national assessments (McGuire, 2022). The key stages were:

- key stage 1: ages 5–7 years,

- key stage 2: ages 8–11 years,

- key stage 3: ages 12–14 years, and

- key stage 4: ages 15–16 years.

(ii) *Levels of attainment,* launched alongside the National Curriculum, specifying standardised, national, age-related expectations of children's achievement. Levels of attainment were devised with the intention of allowing pupils' 'progress' to be measured and school performance evaluated. Levels of attainment were eventually removed, in 2014.

(iii)   *Age-related tests (known as SATS)*, gradually introduced between 1991 and 1995. SATs were to be carried out at ages 7 years, 11 years and 14 years, that is, at the end of key stages 1, 2 and 3. Introduced initially at the end of key stage 1, SATs progressed to key stages 2 and 3 as the first cohort of children moved on.

(iv)   *The new General Certificate of Secondary Education (GCSE) examination*, introduced for 16-year-olds. The teaching to prepare students for GCSE began in 1986, and the first examinations took place in 1988. The GCSE offered one examination for all children, replacing the former 'O' levels (aimed at more able students) and the Certificate of Secondary Education (CSE) (intended for lower attaining pupils). Results of GCSE examinations and SATs were published, so that parents could look at league tables of school performance and compare results to expected national standards. The idea was that parents could assess the effectiveness of schools, and make their choice accordingly (West & Bailey, 2013).

(v)   *New rules on RE and collective worship*, introduced with the 1988 ERA. Maintained schools were required to provide RE and carry out a daily act of collective worship, promoting pupils' moral, spiritual and cultural development (Gillard, 2018).

(vi)   *LMS*, allowing schools to opt out of LEA control, and run themselves as autonomous, GM schools. With funding direct from central government, LMS ostensibly offered schools the flexibility to make their own financial decisions in order to 'respond to the market' (Whitty, 2008, p. 168). GM schools controlled their own budget and resources, took ownership of school buildings and land, and made decisions about pupil admissions and staffing (Fan & Liang, 2020). More than 1,100 primary and secondary schools opted to become GM between 1988 and 1997 (Fan & Liang, 2020), and the majority of the LEAs' schooling budget was devolved to schools. LEAs' spending power was considerably eroded, and the support they had previously been able to offer schools diminished.

    The amount devolved to each school was largely determined by the number and ages of pupils on the school roll, placing schools in a position of having to compete with each other to attract pupils and stay afloat.

Emphasis was placed on 'parent power' (Fisher, 2008, p. 257), and the principle of increased choice for parents in the selection of their children's schools. Open enrolment meant that families were now entitled to express a preference for any school. School profiles no longer strictly reflected the local community and traditional intake area. This meant in practice that wealthier, more informed and educated parents had more choices in selecting a school for their children. They were typically better placed than less-affluent and less-educated parents to research and commute to higher performing schools, and/or to relocate to be near their chosen schools.

(vii) *The establishment of City Technology Colleges (CTCs)*, modelled on fee-paying, independent schools and established in urban areas (Fisher, 2008). CTCs were intended to cater for pupils of all abilities, specialising in science, technology and mathematics. The CTCs were controlled directly by the central government, so taken out of LEA control. A proportion of costs were provided by business sponsors. This model paved the way for the introduction of academies further down the line.

(viii) *A set of National Strategies* (1997–2011). Described as 'one of the most ambitious change management programmes in education' (DfE, 2011, p. 2), the National Strategies provided training and support to schools and teachers in an attempt to raise standards through changes in the way core subjects were taught. The National Strategies took the form of a fixed term programme of interventions, of which the foci included:

- early years and key stage 1,

- primary literacy and numeracy,

- primary school improvement,

- secondary English, mathematics and science,

- secondary school improvement,

- school improvement partners,

- behaviour and attendance,

- narrowing the gaps,

- gifted and talented, and

- Special Educational Needs and Disability (SEND).

The DfE (2011, p. 3) asserts that the National Strategies programme 'was designed to achieve accelerated improvement in standards and to support a professional dialogue about teaching and learning by building teacher confidence in key areas'.

Ofsted

Five years on from the ERA (1988), Ofsted was established, and has endured. Ofsted is the non-ministerial, government department responsible for inspecting educational services. Ofsted replaced the former body responsible for school inspection, HMI, marking a lasting change in the culture and practices of inspection. There were some continuities in the approach of HMI and Ofsted, in that both bodies provided ministers with what Lee and Fitz (1997, p. 39) term 'commentary on the health of the system'. There were also key differences, notably that Ofsted publishes and makes available to the general public information about the performance of individual schools, evaluated against inspection criteria (Lee & Fitz, 1997). The demise of HMI, whose role had largely been seen as supportive and developmental (Baxter, 2013), and the inception of Ofsted, marked a significant shift in the culture of inspection in England.

HMI had been viewed by schools and teachers as 'a trusted critical friend' (Brighouse & Waters, 2022, p. 513), adopting a 'professionally trusting' (Brighouse & Waters, 2022, p. 21) approach. HMI's reports and advice had a significant impact on policy (Lee & Fitz, 1997) and on practice (Brighouse & Waters, 2022) during the 1980s. For example, two major surveys of schools (Primary and Secondary) undertaken by HMI became baseline documents, highly valued by practitioners, and drawn on by ministers in devising policy on curriculum, quality and standards (Lee & Fitz, 1997). Based on inspectors' classroom observations conducted towards the end of the 1970s, the documents contained statements about what constituted good practice. The HMI 'Curriculum Matters' pamphlets then set out a series of curriculum proposals that became the core of National Curriculum (Lee & Fitz, 1997).

Although the relationship between HMI and teachers may have been based on trust, governments of the late 1980s and early 1990s considered HMI to be 'elitist', and 'more focused on influencing government than on schools' (Baxter, Grek, & Segerholm, 2015, p. 80). In England as well as internationally, school inspection was becoming more politicised, and education policy and inspection more closely linked (Baxter, 2013; Baxter et al., 2015). Influenced by international comparisons such as the Programme for International Student Assessment (PISA), politicians realised that 'if education was to be a political vote winner, then the government needed to be seen as tough on education' (Baxter et al., 2015, p. 78). The Conservative government introduced competition in the provision of inspection, in a bid to change the culture of the inspection workforce and take control away from what they perceived to be a too powerful educational establishment (Baxter et al., 2015). As the responsibility for inspection moved from one organisation to the other, there was radical change in 'the personnel, mode of inspection and the direction of the results of inspection' (Lee & Fitz, 1997, p. 39).

With regard to personnel, it had previously been quite commonplace in England for HMI inspections to be carried out by the same LEA advisors with whom teachers worked periodically throughout the year. HMI inspectors, especially those with responsibility for and expertise in particular subjects at secondary level, built positive working relationships with teachers in schools. This meant that the HMI inspectors were able to position themselves centrally to work with schools in the region, and so to create and maintain what Lee and Fitz (1997, p. 47) term 'an interpretative community'. These largely local communities shared many of the characteristics identified in Ehren and Baxter's (2021, p. 43) 'network' model of governance, being 'based on interdependency, trust and empathy [...] [and] most effective when provision cannot be standardized and local actors need a degree of autonomy and flexibility to coordinate their work'. Consistent with the network model, HMI placed support for teachers and schools at the centre. Strong working relationships between teachers and LEA advisors/inspectors were underpinned by mutual trust and a shared set of values founded on a commitment to improving classroom practice. Inspectors and advisors worked to foster collaboration across the borough, whilst teachers maintained the freedom to define for themselves, often in collaboration with neighbouring schools, curricula and pedagogies to best serve the communities in which they worked, and the students they knew. This was no longer the case once HMI were subsumed into and replaced by Ofsted, and responsibility for inspection shifted from local to national level (Baxter et al., 2015).

Under Ofsted, each school is inspected by a contracted team of inspectors assembled for each inspection, and led by Ofsted Registered Inspectors (RIs). The contracted teams comprise a range of people generally not known to the schools. Under the guidance of the RI, the team is required to make a judgement about the quality of educational provision offered by the school. The school will normally be given one day's notice before the Ofsted inspection takes place, and is accorded one of the following grades on completion of the inspection:

- Grade 1: Outstanding.

- Grade 2: Good.

- Grade 3: Requires improvement.

- Grade 4: Inadequate. A school graded as 'inadequate' will normally be subject to a repeat inspection, usually within three years. The school will be expected to make improvements by the time of the follow-up inspection.

Special Measures: This is not an official grade *per se*, but an unofficial classification (Anilkumar, 2023), accorded to schools that receive grade 4 in most of the categories inspected. Schools placed in Special Measures face direct intervention from Ofsted, and are given an action plan for improvement. The schools are then regularly monitored to check whether they are on course to improve. If deemed necessary, Ofsted-approved consultants from outside the school ('Superheads') are brought in (Anilkumar, 2023).

The move from HMI to Ofsted reflects a change in the culture and foundation of schooling in the 1980s and 1990s, and a shift from what Ehren and Baxter (2021, p. 31) term a 'network' to a '(quasi) market-based system' (p. 38), entailing radical restructuring of the schools sector in England.

The government's rationale for wide-scale restructuring of schooling was that marketisation, competition and centralisation would improve schools' performance and ensure quality of education for all. As Ehren and Baxter (2021, pp. 38–39) explain:

> advocates of quasi-markets argue that competition and choice will lead to increased diversity of provision, better and more efficient management of schools and enhanced professionalism and school effectiveness. Marketization is expected to bring particular benefits for families from disadvantaged communities, who have been ill-served by more conventional arrangements. The justifying belief is one of superiority of the private sector in driving up standards, compared with public institutions.

The government's aim was to raise standards by forcing 'underperforming' schools to improve their test and examination results (Fisher, 2008, p. 257). Their strategy was to increase differentiation in the types of schools available (Whitty, 2008), offering different types of educational provision 'to reflect different educational values and purposes and meet the differing needs of pupils' (Woods & Simkins, 2014, p. 326).

As a part of this increased differentiation, the Academies Act (2010) ostensibly offered schools greater freedom and autonomy, building on the earlier precedents set by LMS, GM schools and CTCs, through academisation. Modelled on the USA Charter Schools system, academisation is the process by which state-funded schools move out of LEA control and into the control of private organisations (charitable trusts). When a school converts to academy status, funding is provided directly by the national government, rather than the LEA. Charitable trusts can run a single academy, or multiple schools (known as Multi Academy Trusts, or MATs), the latter having become the dominant model over the last decade. MATs have the autonomy to make their own curricular, financial, staffing and governance decisions (Dunn, 2019), including the freedom to employ teachers who have not been through England's process for teacher certification (Greaney, 2015). Academy chains can be run by a range of possible organisations, the most common now being other successful schools (Greaney, 2015).

The Academies Act offers schools rated 'Good' or 'Outstanding' by Ofsted the option to become an academy. Schools accorded a 'Requires Improvement' grade by Ofsted, on the other hand, are *obliged* to become academies, and are usually taken over by a 'high performing' MAT. Schools are therefore placed under pressure to ensure they are not deemed by Ofsted to be underperforming, as they risk facing punitive measures from centralised government, including closure, direct intervention and forced academisation (McGuire, 2022). For some schools, Ofsted inspection is potentially, therefore, 'a high risk activity' (Baxter, 2013, p. 481), entailing loss of autonomy for schools and leaders (Baxter, 2013).

The shift in inspection regimes signifies a move in English education from a developmental and supportive inspectorate to a punitive model, embodied in Ofsted, whose role is to judge rather than advise or support schools. As the teachers' reflections discussed later in this book reveal, the impact of Ofsted on their work has been considerable, and arguably the single-most detrimental of a succession of reforms.

In the chapters that follow, I discuss the impact of the succession of reforms since 1988 on schooling and teachers' work, and consider why teachers remain in the profession despite the cultural turn and its impact on their daily work in schools. The teachers' career histories and reflections reveal that despite changes in the culture and policy landscape of English education, the teachers have remained committed to the values that underpin their choice of profession, and developed strategies to take back control in an era characterised by prescription and punitive accountability. I conclude by presenting a model of an ideal type of the career-long teacher, adding new understandings of the factors supporting the longevity of a generation of educators in a challenging profession.

NOTES

1. The attrition rate over a number of years of service is shown in Table 1. Significantly, this table shows that there is a trend for this rate to be similar between cohorts. For example, of those teachers qualifying in the period 1996–2011, with potentially 10 years' service, the attrition rate is 35–40%.

2. During the 30 years covered by this book (1988–2018), there were four consecutive governments in power in the UK:

- 1988–1997: Conservative Government (Prime Ministers: Margaret Thatcher & John Major);

- 1997–2010: Labour Government (Prime Ministers: Tony Blair & Gordon Brown);

- 2010–2015: Conservative–Liberal Democrat Coalition Government (Prime Minister: David Cameron – Conservative & Deputy Prime Minister: Nick Clegg – Liberal Democrat); and

- 2015–2018: Conservative Government (Prime Ministers: David Cameron & Theresa May).

Chapter 2

IMPACT OF POLICY SHIFT ON TEACHERS' WORK

INTRODUCTION

The succession of reforms since 1988 (see Gillard, 2018, and Table 2), and the results-driven, efficiency discourse that has evolved in schooling, have had profound implications for teachers' work both in the English state sector (Troman, 2007) and internationally. I focus in this book on teachers working in schools in England.[1] I consider in this chapter literature pertaining to key aspects of the policy-led changes in the nature of teachers' work since 1988. The discussion focusses on (i) competition, accountability and teacher professionalism, (ii) changes and conflicts for teachers and (iii) workload and pressures on teachers.

COMPETITION, ACCOUNTABILITY AND TEACHER PROFESSIONALISM

The belief that increased competition (Green, 2011) leads to greater efficiency in schooling has affected a cultural shift in English education, echoed in countries around the world. Individual institutions, rather than the state, are now positioned as responsible for schooling, and an international focus on measurement of outcomes has led to a preoccupation with comparisons between schools and countries (Biesta, 2009). Global education has become reduced to 'a single space of comparative and commensurate measurement of the performance of school systems' (Lingard, Martino, & Rezai-Rashti, 2013, p. 539). This 'single space' is reflected, for example, in the PISA tables. Sahlberg (2012) terms this widespread shift in perspective and policy the Global Education Reform Movement (GERM).

GERM is rooted in fundamental shifts in the perceived purpose of schooling. It is at least in part underpinned by a belief that education should act as the servant of the economy, creating well-educated and trained individuals for the job market. Resonating with the then Labour Prime Minister Callaghan's (1976) comments, cited in Chapter 1, education is viewed from this perspective as an economic weapon to attract inward investment. Sugrue (2006), for example, argues that the explicit link between economy and education has driven educational change in Ireland. The linking of education and economy has led to the perception that efficiency is the main driver in educational policy and practice.

Within this culture of efficiency and competition, high stakes testing (such as Standard Attainment Tests or SATS) has become a major policy driving schools, defining goals, curricula and the nature of teachers' work (Stevenson & Wood, 2013). The dominant school model is now the 'high performance learning organization' (Fielding, 2006, p. 348), in which the worth and significance of students and teachers rest primarily in 'their contribution, usually via high stakes testing, to the public performance of the organisation' (Fielding, 2006, p. 348). Test and examination results are seen to be a measure of efficiency and effectiveness, as there is an assumed link between student results and the quality of teachers (Labaree, 2011). School leaders in this market-driven environment have little option but to place emphasis on 'precision of targets and delivery' (Fielding, 2006, p. 364). Teachers, in turn, are placed under pressure to prioritise preparing children to pass tests, and held accountable for results.

Accountability in the context of education is not an easy concept to define. At the level of policy governance, accountability has come to have a particular meaning, associated with satisfactory audit (Green, 2011), and entailing the establishment of official structures to carry out such audits. In England, this is the role of Ofsted. Policy-led accountability has impacted the way in which teachers' work is understood. It has led to the introduction of systems of official teachers' standards, giving an explicit framework for what teachers should know, how they should act, and hence, how they should develop their expertise over time. By binding such frameworks together with examination outcomes and the need for efficiency, performance management has become a central point in the accountability system for teachers. By incorporating teachers' standards into this system, teacher professionalism has become a formal, policy-driven process.

Yet, Evans (2011, p. 851) questions the extent to which teacher professionalism can, in reality, be shaped by 'government-imposed reform', commenting that the professionalism 'enacted' by teachers may be quite different from that 'demanded' by the government. The teachers' standards define the government's view of teacher professionalism. This definition, Evans (2011, p. 861) notes, is limited mainly to statements about teachers' behaviour, depicting 'a professionalism that is focussed predominantly on what teachers do, rather than what they think and what attitudes they hold' (Evans, 2011, p. 861). There is little reference in the standards, for instance, to the need for teachers to 'analyse and rationalise their practice' (Evans, 2011, p. 861). The implication of Evans' (2011) analysis is that the professionalism as detailed in the teachers' standards fails to embrace the complexity and sophistication of the lived reality of teachers' work in the classroom. She concludes that only '"enacted" professionalism [...] may be considered to reflect "reality"' (Evans, 2011, p. 862). In the light of Evans' (2011) theory, I consider in Chapter 6 the reality of the professionalism enacted by the teachers in this study, as they navigate the changes and challenges of working in a shifting policy context.

CHANGES AND CONFLICTS FOR TEACHERS

Career-long teachers may experience conflicts as they find themselves working in a context of competing discourses (see, e.g., Craft & Jeffrey, 2008; Fielding, 2006). The target-driven, results-focussed culture that has characterised post-1988 schooling in England contrasts with more nurturing systems in which the focus is on improving teaching (Stigler & Hiebert, 1999), and care of students, rather than competition and efficiency. In such a context, teachers may experience tensions in navigating a contradictory policy/practice landscape. Ball (2003, p. 218) calls this 'values schizophrenia'.

This 'schizophrenia' is at the root of the ethical dilemmas with which teachers have to grapple in making sense of, mediating and implementing reforms, dilemmas which are particularly acute if they involve 'compliance with a policy that conflicts with their concerns for their students' (Schmidt & Datnow, 2005, p. 951). Policy enactment, Schmidt and Datnow (2005) argue, is complex, mediated through teachers' experience and values. Many teachers are committed to an ethic of care (Gilligan, 1982; Reid, 2018; Smith, 2008) towards their students. Therefore, if the teachers can see that a change has a positive impact on their students, they will tend to have a more positive attitude to the policy being introduced (Schmidt & Datnow, 2005). Teachers' prior experiences, beliefs, values and emotions inform how they interpret, evaluate and implement policy, and how they decide what they are comfortable in advocating as professional practice (Schmidt & Datnow, 2005). When suggested changes fit with values and prior knowledge and experience, they will have a good chance of being embedded in practice; where they do not, they will tend to be resisted. As well as values and experience, teacher agency within the organisation, which Gu (2014) links to career phase, has a direct bearing on the way teachers engage with reform. As I discuss in Chapters 7 and 8, for the teachers in this study, teacher agency and commitment to their values emerged as central to their career longevity and readiness to embrace beneficial change.

Teachers' engagement with reform is also linked to what they see to be the scope they have to take ownership and control of the change being implemented. As Kanter (1983, p. 64) asserts, 'change is disturbing when it is done to us, exhilarating when it is done by us [and] considered positive when we are active contributors [...] bringing about something that we desire'. Mediating change, underpinned by a commitment to an ethic of care, may help sustain experienced teachers and encourage them to stay in the profession.

Enforced change may, for others, on the other hand, provide a reason to leave. It seems reasonable to assume that teacher attrition may be, at least in part, a function of teachers' rejection of and resistance to marketisation and competition in schooling. Certainly, this culture has attracted many high-profile critics amongst scholars of education (including Ball, 2003; Biesta, 2009), who express concern about the damaging effects of rising accountability in the school system, and the impact on teachers' workload. I turn in the section below to the issue of workload and pressure on teachers.

WORKLOAD AND PRESSURE ON TEACHERS

Constant increases in the need to service accountability measures, such as being 'Ofsted ready' and ensuring results, have led to increasing workloads (Day & Smethem, 2009) and work intensification for teachers. In the USA context, Valli and Buese (2007) note a shift in teacher roles, with both extensification and intensification of work. The extensification is identified by the constant rise in activities which need to be completed outside of the classroom: new curricula to be planned, increasing levels of testing and the need to record all aspects of teacher work so as to make it available for accountability purposes. Intensification has also occurred, with ever-greater drives towards efficiency in how time is used, leading to teachers feeling constantly time pressured. Some of these patterns are discernible in England, with teachers now spending more of their time on activities outside of teaching than with their students (DfE, 2017).

Several researchers point out the potential negative impacts that accountability-related pressures can precipitate. Berryhill, Linney, and Fromewick (2009), working in the USA, for example, make a link between increases in accountability processes and teacher burnout. They argue that increased accountability creates a constant level of high pressure from which there is no escape. Over time this can lead to feelings of ineffectiveness, exhaustion, lack of fulfilment and being emotionally drained, all symptoms of burnout.

They make the case that these feelings tend to have one or both of two caus-es. The first is role conflict where teachers believe the aims they are being asked to meet are incompatible with each other, leading to exhaustion as they attempt to make them fit. The second is a lack of self-efficacy. Where teach-ers are constantly operating under the direction of others, they have little opportunity to show and develop their own professionalism. This can lead to demotivation and a feeling of time pressure (Wood, 2019). Yet, where teach-ers are given greater levels of autonomy, they actually begin to work harder and longer hours as they are motivated by the work they have identified as being important to them and their students.

This intensification of workload has resulted in an erosion of teacher autonomy and exacerbated feelings of time pressure, which can lead to demo-tivation. This may, in part, explain why attrition rates have remained consist-ently high in the teaching profession in recent years (see Table 1). On the other hand, the data show that the retention rate of teachers is consistent, raising the question of why so many teachers remain. It may be, as Day and Smethem (2009) suggest, that the damaging effects of the contemporary cul-ture of schooling are not ubiquitously experienced. Some teachers, they argue, are content with the culture in which they work, particularly younger teach-ers, who have no alternative with which to compare their experiences. After all, novice teachers in their mid-twenties have only ever known the post-1988 world of education. This does not, though, account for why some teachers remain throughout their working lives. In the later chapters of this book, I present findings emerging from this study to account for how the career-long teachers in this study found ways to navigate the shifting policy landscape, and to remain in post.

In Chapter 3, I turn to the literature and research on teacher retention, and explore some of the factors that seem to encourage and enable teachers to stay long-term in the teaching profession despite the context of constantly changing policy.

NOTE

1. The four nations of the UK (England, Wales, Scotland and Northern Ireland) each has its own education system and its own National Curriculum, and there is some variation in the qualifications offered to children. This book is based solely on the English state system.

Chapter 3

TEACHER RETENTION:
UNDERSTANDING WHY THEY STAY

INTRODUCTION

Research into the reasons why teachers choose to enter, stay in or leave the teaching profession identifies a complex, multidimensional range of factors that frame and influence their career decisions. The factors identified include, for example, the teachers' passion for teaching (Day, 2004); their emotional ties to their schools (McIntyre, 2010); and the nature of the settings in which they work (Gu & Day, 2013). In this chapter, I consider the literature associated with teacher longevity in the profession under the headings: (i) teacher motivation and job satisfaction, (ii) institutional factors and (iii) teacher compliance.

TEACHER MOTIVATION AND JOB SATISFACTION

Where recruitment and retention are considered, the focus often tends to be on job satisfaction and the nature of teachers' motivation, with motivation being characterised as either intrinsic/altruistic, or extrinsic (e.g., Chiong, Menzies, & Parameshwaran, 2017; Han & Yin, 2016). Relatively little attention is given to extrinsic forms of motivation, although Chiong et al. (2017) note that instrumental incentives, such as holidays and pay, can help to retain experienced teachers. For the most part, intrinsic/altruistic forms of motivation are seen to predominate (see, e.g., Chiong et al., 2017; Perrachione, Rosser, & Petersen, 2008; Six, 2021), and include love of subject, caring and wanting to make a difference to students and society (Hobbs, 2012; Kyriacou & Coulthard, 2000).

Making a difference to students appears to be viewed as more important than making a contribution to society. This is particularly the case for early career teachers, although Chiong et al. (2017) note that both of these sources of intrinsic motivation strengthen with years of experience. A combination of altruism and a strong sense of their own 'professional mastery' (Chiong et al., 2017, p. 1083) seems to encourage experienced teachers to stay in the profession long term. Over time, experienced educators develop a sense of self-efficacy, that is, 'the self-belief of teachers that they can exert a positive effect on their students' (Day, 2004, p. 72). This self-belief is influential in securing their long-term commitment to the profession.

INSTITUTIONAL FACTORS

It is quite well documented that teachers' commitment, and their vocationally orientated, altruistic and caring motivations, can be supported or undermined by a range of institutional factors (Chiong et al., 2017). These institutional factors include workload (Skaalvik & Skaalvik, 2017), pupil behaviour (Fernet, Guay, Senécal, & Austin, 2012), high stakes accountability (Ryan et al., 2017), leadership (Mancuso, Roberts, & White, 2011), trust (Six, 2021) and the nature of the school culture (Dumay & Galand, 2011). Cultures of collaboration (Ovenden-Hope, Blandford, Cain, & Maxwell, 2018; Weiss, 1999) and collegiality (Shah & Abualrob, 2012) seem to be more likely to secure teachers' enduring commitment and to encourage them to stay. Leadership that fosters, encourages and facilitates such institutional cultures is therefore very important in ensuring continuity and retention of staff (Day et al., 2007; Ingersoll & Smith, 2003; Szczesiul & Huizenga, 2014).

The importance of institutional culture is also emphasised in some of the literature on teacher resilience, signifying a move away from the notion that resilience 'resides largely within a person' (Gu, 2014, p. 508). Instead, it is recognised that teachers experience their working lives in the space in which school culture and the social relationships of a school interplay. Consideration is given to the interplay of personal dispositions (such as the sense of calling, motivation and self-efficacy) with contextual, support structures (see Ainsworth & Oldfield, 2019; Boldrini, Sappa, & Aprea, 2019; Day, 2008; Day & Hong, 2016; Gu, 2014). Typically, the support structures identified are multilayered, and include collegiality, relationships with school leaders and colleagues, and teacher learning communities. Setting out three characteristics of teacher resilience therefore as 'context specific', 'role-specific' and 'personal', Gu (2014, p. 508) highlights the role played by relationships in fostering resilience and ensuring that teachers' commitment and motivation are sustained.

In trying to understand how institutional factors can affect teachers' likelihood of staying in the profession career-long, it is helpful to consider George's (2009) notion of the 'psychological contract'. Essentially, the psychological contract is part of an unwritten, tacit agreement between the employee and their employer. The psychological contract, the detail of which is implicit, constitutes an assumed understanding of mutual employee–employer expectations. It is quite separate from the formal contract of employment, in which duties and responsibilities are stipulated. George (2009, p. 11) identifies two types of psychological contract: transactional and relational. The focus of transactional contracts is 'mainly economic' (George, 2009, p. 11), whereas relational contracts have 'both an economic and an emotional focus' (George, 2009, p. 11). The relational contract is specific to the individual teacher, and typically includes 'a personal identification with their organization' (George, 2009, p. 13). It is dynamic, evolving over the course of the employee's career, and the employee's commitment to the organisation is 'open-ended with respect to time frames' (George, 2009, p. 13). It is only when and if the employee perceives that the employer has broken their commitment to the contract that the employee's motivation and identification with the organisation are altered or undermined.

TEACHER COMPLIANCE

Teachers' capacity and willingness to adapt professional practices in response to policy imperatives may also be a factor enabling their continued commitment to the profession. Craft and Jeffrey (2008, p. 1) acknowledge that policy change post-1988 initially caused teachers 'considerable stress'. Significant shifts in the policy landscape meant that '[teachers'] professional status was reconstructed, contemporary pedagogic values of creative teaching were marginalised by a performativity discourse and professional commitment came under strain' (Craft & Jeffrey, 2008, p. 1). Some teachers experienced 'inner conflicts [and] inauthenticity' (Ball, 2003, p. 215), and the decision taken by some to quit the profession has been viewed by some writers as resistance (e.g., Glazer, 2018). It is argued that, for those who remain, resistance is not an option, and therefore, over time, teachers have had to learn to 'adapt their substantial selves' (Troman, 2007, p. 8), by finding a way to reach a compromise between their values and delivery of the required objectives (Craft & Jeffrey, 2008).

Considering the evidence of compromise, it is interesting to note how the anxiety and resistance that characterised teachers' immediate reaction to post-1988 reform in England seemed gradually to give way to pragmatic accommodation. Studies in the first decade of the 21st century 'showed adaptations to the situation with some unique appropriations of performativity' (Craft & Jeffrey, 2008, p. 1). Teachers were said to be less 'opposed to inspection and annual testing' (Craft & Jeffrey, 2008, p. 20) than they had been in the past. It is argued that achieving good scores in tests was viewed by teachers as rewarding, and as evidence that they were 'making a difference' (Troman, 2007, p. 4). This affirmation made them feel special and raised their status in the eyes of colleagues (Troman, 2007). Similarly, Ball (2003, pp. 218–219) argues that the '"incentives" of performance' provided 'a new basis for ethical decision making and moral judgement': teachers learn that they 'can become more than [they] were and be better than others – [they] can be "outstanding," "successful," "above the average"'. Such considerations would suggest that the teachers who remain in the profession have come to embrace and assimilate the principles of the new era in education, although as I show later in this book, this is something of an oversimplification of the case.

It is also argued that apparent compliance with the post-1988 culture and ways of thinking about teaching and learning is reflected, too, in the shifting language of educational discourses. Craft and Jeffrey (2008, p. 20) identify a 'powerful performative progression "narrative" in which teachers and pupils [celebrate] individual and class incremental movement from one grade or level to the next'. The language of performativity, they argue, has been incorporated into teachers' practice so that it has become 'the discourse of the school, the staff room and the classroom'. Teachers, Ball (2003, p. 218) holds, have learned 'to talk about [themselves] and the relationships, purposes and motivations in these new ways'. Through these new ways of talking, shared values are negotiated and adjusted, helping to secure teachers' commitment to the team and the institution (Craft & Jeffrey, 2008, p. 4). It may be that this capacity to adapt in this context is a factor in teachers' longevity in the profession, although as I discuss in the later chapters of this book, it does not necessarily mean teachers lose sight of the main motivating factors that drive them, such as making a difference to children's lives.

This study focussed on some of the many teachers at the upper end of the age range, who had remained long term in the profession in an era when there have been multiple changes in policy. Their enduring commitment suggests some capacity to accommodate and adapt to policy shift. However, as discussed in Chapters 7 and 8, the ways in which the teachers in this study adapted involved mediation of externally imposed imperatives to suit their working contexts, underpinned by their values and commitment to students. They took ownership of change implementation in their schools and classrooms. This study therefore offers fresh perspectives on longevity and retention in the teaching profession, shedding light on the importance of teacher agency in highly prescriptive policy contexts.

In Chapter 4, I explain how the study was conducted, before presenting vignettes of the nine teachers who were involved.

Chapter 4

METHODOLOGY: GATHERING CAREER HISTORY NARRATIVES

INTRODUCTION

As discussed in Chapter 1, the post-1988 era in England has been characterised by a succession of educational policy changes, and a consequent shift in the culture of schooling. I wanted to understand more about the experiences and perceptions of teachers who had worked career-long in this shifting policy and cultural context. Specifically, I wanted to understand how policy shift has been experienced by teachers in the post-1988 era, a largely underresearched generation of teachers. In this chapter, I discuss the research design and the research process my co-researchers and I devised to gather insights into career-long teachers' experiences of implementing the reforms.

A team of four researchers was involved in the data collection phase of the study. Our focus was on how the career-long teachers experienced the impact of the reforms over time, and the factors that contributed to the teachers' longevity in the profession. Data were collected through retrospective, career history interviews, eliciting a unique, longitudinal view of the policy reforms from the perspective of those who had had to implement them. Participants were interviewed during the academic year 2017–2018, approximately 30 years on from the 1988 ERA. Teachers' retrospective reflections afforded insights into their perspectives on the ways in which schooling, and the nature of teachers' work, had evolved over a 30-year period. This book offers new and authentic understandings of a period of socio-educational history unlikely to have been captured otherwise.

This work is significant because the last 30+ years in education have seen reform at an unprecedented rate and pace (for a detailed summary of reforms, see Gillard, 2018), changing the nature of the work of schools and teachers. Drawing on the experiences and perceptions of career-long teachers from primary, secondary and post-compulsory education, the study affords original insights that are critical to understanding this era of reform from the perspective of those who have lived experience of implementing the changes.

RESEARCH QUESTIONS

The purpose of the study was to seek career-long teachers' perceptions of:

(i)   how their daily work had been impacted by changes in educational policy since 1988;

(ii)   the factors that had helped them to sustain their commitment career-long in the profession in this era of change.

The research questions guiding the study were therefore:

(i)   What do career-long teachers perceive to have been the impact of educational policy shift since 1988 on their work?

(ii)   What sense do they make of the factors helping to sustain them career-long in the teaching profession?

RESEARCH DESIGN

The research design was based on the methodological work of psychologists Smith, Flowers, and Larkin (2009) on Interpretative Phenomenological Analysis (IPA). The epistemological foundation of phenomenology is that 'the world, consciousness, perception and lived experience are inseparable, there is not an objective world that exists separately from our perception of it' (Mason, 2018, p. 8). The methodological implication of this worldview is that '[the] researcher needs to explore this interconnectedness' (Mason, 2018, p. 8). In this study, we sought to understand career-long teachers' perceptions of the ways in which their work as teachers had been framed by educational reform over time. Our research design allowed us to gather the teachers' in-depth reflections on their lived experience of implementing reform, including the strategies they adopted and the cultural shifts they experienced in schooling. The participants in the study were well placed to offer their reflections on the ways in which the multiple reforms had affected teachers' work, as they had had to interpret, mediate and implement the policies during the course of their careers. Our assumption as researchers was that our participants were the experts on their own work.

As a phenomenological study, the primary focus of our investigation was on lived experience (see Denscombe, 2010), and we drew on the work of Smith et al. (2009) to inform the research process and analytical strategy. Our aim was to interpret the sense participants seemed to be making of their lived experiences. We engaged therefore in what Smith et al. (2009, p. 3) term 'a double hermeneutic', that is, 'the researcher [...] trying to make sense of the participant trying to make sense of what is happening to them'.

The researcher's sense-making can only be 'second order' (Smith et al., 2009, p. 3), as it is only possible to access participants' experiences through the participants' own accounts. Time and space for reflection during the interviews was therefore important, as these were the moments when participants reflected on their experiences, and the meaning they made of them. When silence naturally occurred during the interviews, we did not, as interviewers, interrupt their pensive moments, but gave participants space for reflection. It is important in research of this nature that interviewers are sufficiently skilled and relaxed to allow silence to happen, and not to fill all available space with talk and questioning, stifling the scope for reflection. The purpose of IPA is to allow researchers to 'engage with those reflections' (Smith et al., 2009, p. 3).

This is a powerful method for researching the sense individuals make of major transition points in their lives. It is noteworthy that IPA has been used, for example, in medical and psychological research into the experiences of stroke survivors (e.g., Connell, McMahon, & Adams, 2014), alcohol and drug users in recovery (Shinebourne & Smith, 2010) and male victims of female-perpetrated intimate partner violence (Morgan & Wells, 2016). In this study, transitions in teachers' working lives are the focus, as participants come to terms with mediating externally mandated change in their daily work in school.

THE SAMPLE POPULATION

My co-researchers and I sought to interview teachers who had been in the profession long term. We invited volunteers aged over 50 years, with 20 or more years' experience, to take part in the study. In order to recruit interviewees, we placed advertisements in the newsletters sent out by our two universities to our partnership schools, that is, schools with whom we worked as Schools of Education to offer initial teacher education. In all, across the

Table 3. Summary of Participants: Roles and Teaching Experience.

Pseudonym	Job/Phase	Teaching Career Started
Anna	Secondary English Teacher Head of Department and Literacy Co-ordinator	1977
Barbara	Primary School Teacher Career-long Classroom Teacher	1977
Cathy	Secondary English and Humanities Teacher Vice Principal	1980
Dan	Secondary School Teacher Head of Science and Co-ordinator for Initial Teacher Training	1988
Edna	Secondary History Teacher	1976
Freda	Secondary Geography Teacher	1977
Gail	Primary School Teacher, within a MAT Modern Foreign Language Co-ordinator Special Needs Co-ordinator Safeguarding Lead	1975
Henry	Secondary School Teacher of Humanities, in an academy	1981
Irene	Sixth Form College Teacher of Humanities Head of Citizenship and Assistant Curriculum Leader	1981

partnerships of two providers, our newsletters went out to over 600 schools. We received 12 responses from teachers willing to participate. The volunteers' actual availability to be interviewed meant that in practice we were able to interview nine teachers. (For a summary of the participants, see Table 3.)

It is usual for IPA studies to be based on a small number of participants, as it is an idiographic approach, involving the 'detailed examination of the particular case' (Smith et al., 2009, p. 3). Smith et al. (2009, p. 3) recommend a maximum of nine participants, as the aim is to 'reveal something of each of those individuals [...] [and to] explore in detail the similarities and differences between each case'. The sample in this study was, as Smith et al. (2009, p.3) recommend, 'reasonably homogeneous', comprising seven women and two men, all over 50 years old, all white British or Europeans, who had been teaching for 20 years or more. The homogeneity of the sample allowed researchers to 'examine convergence and divergence in some detail', within the sample (Smith et al., 2009, p. 3). It is acknowledged that this all-white sample cannot be assumed to be representative of all teachers in England.

The sample comprised three primary school teachers, five secondary teachers and one sixth form college (i.e., post-compulsory) teacher (see Table 3).

Two of the sample mentioned that they worked in an academy or a MAT. Pseudonyms are used throughout to protect the identity of the teachers, and, for the same reasons, the schools, MATs and areas in which they worked are not named. Interviews were conducted in the teachers' schools, at times to suit the participants.

RESEARCH APPROACH AND INTERVIEW STRATEGY

As people experience major events in their lives, they start to reflect on the significance of what they have experienced or are experiencing. IPA research 'aims to engage with these reflections' (Smith et al., 2009, p. 3). The interviews we devised enabled the research team to examine how 'the everyday flow of experience' – in this case teachers' work and the policies that affected it – took on 'a particular significance' for our teacher participants (Smith et al., 2009, p. 1). Following the advice of Smith et al. (2009), we designed a flexible, semi-structured interview schedule as the basis for the interviews. This design was helpful for two reasons. First, we had identified from our readings certain areas we wished to explore (e.g., the implications for teachers of a range of policy changes, workload issues, the impact of accountability and so forth), and our core questions allowed us to investigate some of the specific areas we wished to pursue. Second, the interview design also allowed us the flexibility, through probing, to capture novel, idiosyncratic and original experiences and perceptions. We wanted to avoid pre-empting responses or leading interviewees. In order to afford them the scope to identify for themselves what, in their experience, the key policies and impacts had been, our questioning was expressly open-ended.

During the interviews, participants talked about particular experiences relating to policy and policy implementation that for them, had significance. In some cases, the examples they cited took the form of critical incidents, changing the nature of their work in ways that could not be reversed, or prompting them to think and act differently thereafter. The open-ended design of the interview questioning allowed for findings to be harnessed that were complex, contradictory and in some cases, unexpected. Our interview design enabled us to delve deeper into individual stories, without losing sight of the overall purpose in interviewing this particular group of career-long teachers. These individual perspectives are important not just in understanding idiosyncrasies but, essentially, can provide insights into the essence of the experiences of the wider group.

Prior to the interview, we sent out to participants information letters, in which the purpose of the study was explained. Participants were asked to think through the main changes that had taken place in terms of policy that affected their work, and to bring to the interview a few notes of the key changes, to aid their discussion in the interview. We deliberately avoided highlighting particular policies so that the teachers could identify for themselves what had been the key influences framing their experiences. In addition, we asked them to prepare to talk us through their biographical background in terms of an outline of their career (positions held, schools, etc.). Some participants brought a CV to aid this discussion, some used notes, others worked from memory. The core interview questions were based on the following guide schedule:

Biographical background

> How long have you been teaching?
>
> Outline of career, positions and schools.
>
> What drew you to teaching?
>
> Where did you start ... initial impressions ... expectations of career?

Exploration of policy-led changes to work

> Reflecting back on your career how would you describe the experience in terms of the changes you have seen? Positive/negative policy changes in terms of impact on your work?
>
> How effective was the quality of support provided for educational developments/initiatives; notions of what was effective/ineffective?

Exploration of career trajectory

> How do you feel about your personal career?
>
> How do you experience that at this point in time?
>
> Have there been times when you have been more/less positive during your career and why?
>
> How far were career aspirations met?
>
> If you went back to a particular point in time, what might you change, in terms of policy reform?
>
> What do you aspire to now?

Additional questions

> What have you valued/do you value most in colleagues?
>
> What do you think makes a successful school?

To explore more deeply, we asked probing questions as needed in order to allow individual accounts to emerge. This is an important aspect of the research design. Our methods were sufficiently rigorous to allow us to elicit comparable data and identify cross-sample themes, and sufficiently flexible to harness complexity, contradiction and divergence. We devised a research design that would enable us to gather more profound understandings of the multifarious ways in which policy framed and influenced individual teachers' work, and to investigate the ways in which the teachers mediated and implemented policy. In many instances, the 'probing' merely took the form of acknowledging the participant's comments and giving minimal verbal cues to add more detail (Uhuh? Yeah? Really? It was? Hmmm, etc.). At other points the questions became more targeted (e.g., so this was in the eighties? What then? How did it affect you personally? What happened later?, etc.). This allowed detailed, complex accounts to be gathered. We were interested both in individual stories and the commonalities, where they emerged, across the sample or sections of the sample. It was important that our approach to organising and analysing the data took account of both aims, as we discuss below.

DATA ANALYSIS STRATEGY

In order to ensure we were as faithful as possible to the accounts provided by our participants, we ensured all interviews were fully transcribed. The layout of the transcriptions was such that wide margins were provided on each side of the transcript to allow space for annotation. This was an important element in our data analysis. The interview transcripts were 'analysed case by case through a systematic, qualitative analysis' (Smith et al., 2009, p. 4). We began by looking individually, as the four researchers involved, at the nine transcripts. Initially, working alone, we read the transcripts and merely noted in the margin anything interesting as we progressed through. This might be, for instance, the participant's reflections on a particular policy, or their account of how they had come to interpret and implement a policy or how it had changed their work or understanding. The emphasis at this point was squarely on looking in detail at the individual transcript and identifying themes within the narrative, as recommended by Smith et al. (2009). We each read the nine transcripts several times before coming together as a team to discuss what seemed to be emerging from the narratives. We were able to pool our observations to identify a (very) long list of themes that had relevance for individuals or in some cases for a number of individuals in the sample group. Some of the identifiable themes at that stage included, for example:

- issues around time and the speed at which policy changed and had to be implemented;

- perceptions and experiences of generic and particular policy shift;

- perceptions of National Curriculum and levels of attainment; and

- negative/positive/mixed perceptions and experiences of Ofsted.

At this stage we did not seek to reduce, or abstract from, these multiple themes. We did not want the search for cross-sample themes to become the main focus, such that individual perspectives were obscured. Our team meetings to discuss the in-narrative themes were lengthy and detailed, and we tried to keep the focus on lived experience rather than attempting to theorise. The list of themes was at this stage unwieldy, however, and needed some honing to provide a coherent basis for ascertaining and reporting findings. We worked then to cluster the themes we had identified into larger groupings, under new headings, or 'super-ordinate' themes (Smith et al., 2009, p. 96). At this stage, there was a need to engage in a level of abstraction to gain some clarity in what the data told us. We then needed to collapse certain super-ordinate themes to a new level of abstraction. The final version of the super-ordinate themes, organised under the two research questions, is detailed below. Findings are discussed in Chapters 6 and 7, under the super-ordinate thematic headings.

Super-ordinate Themes

RQ1. What do career-long teachers perceive to have been the impact of educational policy shift since 1988 on their work?

Although the participants' versions of events differed, four super-ordinate themes were clearly identified as emerging from all nine narratives. The impact of policy shift since 1988 was seen to have entailed:

- An erosion of teachers' professional freedom, with increased prescription and accountability.

- Increased workload and pressure on teachers, and long working hours.

- Changes in the culture of schooling and the nature of teaching.

- Increased challenges resulting from the changes.

> RQ2. *What sense do they make of the factors helping to sustain them career-long in the teaching profession?*

By looking not just at what they said but at how they talked about it, we were able to ascertain how the teachers made sense of the combination of factors that had sustained them long term in the teaching profession in this era of shifting policy. We identified the following as key factors:

- Their sense of agency and ability to take control of change.

- Their appreciation of positive relationships in school.

- Their sustained commitment to making a difference/student success.

- Their concern to maintain a work/life balance.

POSITIONALITY

Three colleagues and I were involved in collecting data for this project. Three of us were already school teachers when the ERA (1988) came into being, and all four of us are over 50 years old. Although we all left the teaching profession to become initial teacher educators, we have much in common with the teachers we interviewed in terms of background, values, ideas about education, social justice and so on. We cannot claim to be objective or removed from this work. With this in mind, we were committed to ensuring the research process was as rigorous and systematic as possible, so that our beliefs and biases could not lead the findings or cause us to be blinkered to insights we had not expected, or did not like.

We made use of two critical friends at different stages of the process. In the early stages, we worked with a Professor of Education who critiqued our research design, including our research questions, rationale, sampling strategy and so on. He urged us not to seek out our former friends and colleagues in the teaching profession as participants, but to cast the net widely and include teachers we had not met. Inevitably, given our extensive networks, the sample included individuals some of us knew, but we deliberately allocated interviewees so that we as researchers were interviewing teachers we had not met before. This is also a useful tactic in terms of encouraging participants not to assume the interviewer is aware of their story already, but to be explicit in giving full and detailed accounts to the stranger researcher.

We tried to guard against leading behaviour in the interview process, by giving minimal responses and asking only the core questions plus probing as appropriate. We were conscious, too, of the need to keep body language and facial expressions neutral. When we embarked on the annotations of the data, we worked separately, as individuals, before comparing notes. We tried, as Smith et al. (2009) recommend, to 'bracket off' our own knowledge, experience, values and expectations as we made sense of the data. It is, of course, never quite possible to 'bracket off' completely all of the values, expectations, knowledge, emotions and ideas we carry with us professionally and personally. It is important, though, to acknowledge that these exist, and to try to minimise the extent to which they affect the data.

At the same time as acknowledging our biases as researchers, it is worth considering how our positionality might be an asset in the study. In order to make sense of interviewees' understandings of the world, we have to use

> *our own selves, our own knowledge of the world as people*
> *[and] immerse ourselves in the research contexts in which we are*
> *interested – for example, talking to people in depth, attending to*
> *[...] every clue to the meanings that they are investing in something.*
> *(Thomas, 2009, p. 75)*

Having some insider knowledge of the contexts in which the teachers worked, and had worked, gave us an advantage in terms of the conversations we were likely to be able to have in the interviews. Our contextualised, professional knowledge was advantageous in helping us to understand the nuanced set of perceptions we gathered. So, rather than trying to eliminate or ignore this insider knowledge, we valued being able, as Thomas (2009, pp. 75–76) suggests, to 'be a *participant* in [our] research situation and understand it as an insider'. This does not mean that bias is acceptable, but that it needs to be acknowledged and managed so that it works to the benefit rather than the detriment of the study. Our 'insiderness' meant that we could use our own interests and understandings to help interpret and understand the expressed views and behaviour of others. It also meant that we had to bear in mind the impact our positionality would have on the research. As Thomas (2009, p. 76) cautions, as an insider researcher, 'you have to recognise your position – your social background, likes and dislikes, preferences and predilections, political affiliations, class, gender and ethnicity – and how this position [...] is likely to be affecting your interpretation'.

Aware that positionality could affect our interpretation, we worked together as a team to feed back ideas from the data such that we regulated each other, to an extent. We tried to be systematic in looking at what the evidence was, whether the data pointed to the claim being made and so on. Eventually, we were able to tabulate the key themes and show the extent to which each theme had been evident in the account of which participant. We then invited a second critical friend, a research assistant, to join us for a few days and to undertake a thorough cross-check of the data, to confirm or refute the tabular data. She identified where the evidence of the different themes could be found in the narratives, and the relative strength of this body of evidence. She fed back that for the most part, she confirmed our account, although in one or two cases felt we had overstated the strength of the evidence. We therefore modified our claims accordingly to reflect what the data showed rather than what we had expected it to show. The findings discussed in Chapters 6 and 7 are credible, therefore, having been derived from 'qualitative data [that] have been produced and checked in accord with good practice' (Denscombe, 2010, p. 299). Nonetheless, this is a small-scale, exploratory study with a number of limitations, as I acknowledge below.

LIMITATIONS OF THE STUDY

This was a small-scale study involving nine participants. The sample was recruited from a very large pool of teachers, from which only 12 volunteered – even in this respect our participants were not typical of the wider group. It may be that they had a particular motivation urging them to tell their stories to university-based researchers. Moreover, as teachers who had stayed in the profession long term, they at best represented a group who, despite the challenges of a changing policy context, had elected to remain. It is reasonable to assume that the stories we might have gathered from their peers who had chosen to leave pre-retirement age would be quite different. Follow-up research might seek to harness the stories of those teachers who quit, albeit they are likely to be a difficult group to access.

ETHICAL CONSIDERATIONS

Our research team included researchers from two universities, and our research was jointly funded by our two institutions. We therefore were obliged to apply to both universities for permission to carry out the study, which was granted by the ethics committees at both institutions. In conducting the research, we kept the three fundamental principles of consent, honesty and care in mind (Wood & Smith, 2016). First, participants were provided with an information sheet outlining the purpose of the study and an outline of what to expect in the interview. We included how the data from the interview would be used. We explained that care would be taken to protect anonymity, whilst acknowledging that we could not give a watertight guarantee that participants would not be recognised by people who knew them, were their friends, family and colleagues to read our reports or attend our presentations. We were able to reassure participants that pseudonyms would be used, and that their schools and the areas in which they worked would not be identified. It was made clear that participants had the right to withdraw from the study at any point, including after the interviews. No-one did choose to withdraw.

Whilst I describe the interviews we used as 'semi-structured', in the telling, the teachers' stories took on a narrative form as the participants reflected on their career histories. I have written elsewhere (see Smith, 2012; Wood & Smith, 2016) about the ways in which asking participants to reflect on their past lives and memories can prove to be unexpectedly painful or embarrassing for some people. The open-ended nature of narrative styles of interviewing can mean that narrators find themselves talking about memories or aspects of their lives they had not anticipated discussing, which can be upsetting in some cases. We were careful to alert participants that this was a possibility, and that, should they find themselves discussing areas they would prefer not to share, they must feel free to stop, change tack or withdraw completely. We tried to alert them to this possibility without over-dramatising or causing alarm, seeking to reassure rather than to create an expectation that the interview should be highly personal and intrusive. In the event, our participants did not experience upsetting or embarrassing moments in their interviews, as far as we were aware. There were certainly, though, a number of instances of frustration and anger as they discussed the challenges and sources of anxiety in their work. Some examples of these will be included in Chapters 6 and 7, when I discuss the findings emanating from the study.

In Chapter 5, I present vignettes of each of the participants in the study, offering more details of the individual career histories elicited.

Chapter 5

CAREER HISTORIES

INTRODUCTION

This chapter comprises nine vignettes. Each vignette provides a summary outline of each participating teacher's career history and experience. Pseudonyms are used throughout, and other identifiers removed. (See also Table 3, Chapter 4, for a summary of participants' roles and experience.)

ANNA: 'IT'S MY LIFE, IN A WAY'

Anna was a secondary school English teacher whose love of her subject brought her into the profession in 1977, more than a decade before the Education Reform Act (ERA) (1988) and the introduction of the National Curriculum.

Anna completed her training in a college in the north of England, achieving her Certificate of Education (Cert. Ed.), a common route into the teaching profession at the time. She secured a teaching post in a local school, where she stayed for three years. In 1980, following their marriage, she and her husband moved to the Midlands. There Anna found a temporary post, covering a maternity leave. She was subsequently appointed to a Scale 2[1] post as second in department in the school, and has worked there ever since. The school is a 10–16 school, offering key stages 2–4.

When her first child was born, Anna took the standard maternity leave, returning to work full-time thereafter. Two years later, her second child was born. Again, Anna took the normal maternity leave, but this time returned to work afterwards as a part-time teacher, on a job-share basis. Anna and her job-share partner had wanted to share the head of department role, but their headteacher would not allow this. Anna therefore continued as a classroom teacher, ceding the responsibilities and status she had previously held.

When her younger child was nine years old, Anna was offered the opportunity to return to full-time teaching, which she accepted. She again progressed to the post of second in department, and then head of department, a role she still held at the time of the interview. Anna described her role as her 'dream job', talking enthusiastically about how much she enjoyed being Head of English. She saw teaching as a vocation, commenting, 'it's my life, in a way'. She had no intention of moving on from her job and expected to end her career in the school.

Anna recalled a time pre-National Curriculum when teachers were free to decide on curriculum content and pedagogy. She recalled, too, the panic that ensued when the National Strategies[2] were introduced, and teachers felt unsure about what they had to do. She now reflected that instead of panicking, teachers needed to think through what works in their particular context. She acknowledged, though, that it is more difficult than it used to be to just select the 'parts that work'. Overall, Anna considered that there had been 'more positives than negatives' in terms of the impact of policy shift on teachers' work over the last three decades.

BARBARA: 'A CLASS TEACHER THAT WHOLE TIME'

Barbara was a primary school teacher, who, like Anna, had been teaching since 1977. At the time of the interview, she was two weeks away from retirement. Barbara had wanted to become a teacher from an early age, although she acknowledged that, when she left school, there were very few other career options open to girls.

She completed her teacher training in a college in the East of England, obtaining her Cert. Ed. in 1976. Teaching posts were difficult to find at the time, so she applied for and was appointed to the teaching pool in an East Midlands city. This led eventually to her appointment to a primary school teaching post, which she took up in January 1977. She remained in this post for a few years,

*until the birth of her first child. At the time, Barbara explained,
women did not have the option of returning to work part-time after
maternity leave, so had to either return to full-time work, or resign.
In the city in which she was working, however, there was also
the possibility of taking a three-year, unpaid, career break before
returning to teaching in the LEA area. With limited alternatives on
offer, Barbara chose this route to return to teaching.*

*When she returned, she found that resuming her former post
was not an option; only a temporary position could be offered
post-career break. Thus, Barbara's return to teaching was in a
succession of temporary posts. The effect on her career path was
that she did what she termed 'lots of bits and bobs' over a number
of years, including supply teaching. Eventually, she returned to the
school in which she had started her career. By the time Barbara
became pregnant with her second child, the option to take a
three-year, unpaid, career break had been withdrawn, and she found
herself supply teaching again after the birth of her second baby.*

*When her younger child was four years old, Barbara found
a job in a different school, and she has worked there ever since.
She explained that she has been 'a class teacher that whole time',
never having taken on additional responsibilities or been promoted
to a leadership post. She commented that she realised she was quite
unusual, in that there were not many teachers who had remained
classroom teachers for 40 years, without taking on leadership roles.*

*Reflecting on how she had stayed the course in her teaching
career, Barbara described herself as 'resilient' and 'a plodder'.
She explained that she saw her work primarily as 'a job', and
that having her home and family outside the job had helped to
sustain her. She also drew on the support of her other 'family' – her
colleagues in school, who were very important to her. She was
very appreciative of the team work and support that characterised
her school.*

*Barbara had seen a lot of changes during her teaching career.
Like Anna, Barbara recalled that when she started teaching in
1977, she did not have to disclose to others what she was teaching
or planning to teach. However, she added that this meant that,
especially as a new teacher, she really did not know whether what
she was teaching was appropriate. The introduction of the National
Curriculum and levels of attainment were, in Barbara's view, an
improvement, therefore, helping her to feel more certain that*

what she was teaching was appropriate. Overall, Barbara felt, like Anna, that there were more positives than negatives in terms of the policy-led shifts she had experienced during her career.

She remembered that teachers had been very wary of the National Curriculum when it was first introduced. Reflecting back, she explained that, although such major changes can seem quite daunting at first, they become more manageable and flexible in the process of implementation. She described herself as compliant, and willing to do her best to make initiatives work. Such willingness was, for Barbara, a key part of being a member of a school staff team.

CATHY: 'IDEALIST'

Cathy was 62 years old at the time of the interview. She was a Vice-Principal in what she described as 'a very turbulent school'. An English specialist, she had also taught some humanities. She had been teaching since 1980, having worked initially in residential social work and then in a psychiatric hospital. Teaching had not been her first choice of profession. She had wanted to become a social worker, but she recalled that at the time, grants were available for teacher training but not for social work, hence she became a teacher. During her teaching career, she had held a range of middle and senior leadership roles, including subject and pastoral leadership, as well as whole school responsibilities.

Like Anna and Barbara, Cathy recalled a time pre-1988 when teachers were 'in the driving seat', free to make decisions about schemes of work, lessons and resources. She reflected that this freedom brought with it 'really creative, excellent practice'. At the same time, though, it also brought with it 'a lot of gaps and [...] low expectations'.

Cathy acknowledged that many of the policy changes that had taken place during her career had been based on sound ideas. Her experience had been, though, that the changes were unnecessarily bureaucratic and burdensome to implement. She gave the example of the National Curriculum and levels of attainment as particularly bureaucratic and cumbersome. Cathy saw this cumbersome process as the result of changes being designed and led by policymakers who lacked any real understanding of the day-to-day work of schools. At the same time, she acknowledged that the changes had helped to ensure that children were offered a broad and balanced experience.

Cathy reflected that she came from a generation of 'idealists', driven by a commitment to social justice. She aspired to work with children from disadvantaged backgrounds and was motivated to work to help them improve their lives. This aspiration, she explained, continued to motivate her. She remained, overall, very positive about her work.

DAN: 'MAKING A DIFFERENCE'

Dan was 53 years old at the time of the interview. He had been teaching since 1988. Prior to becoming a teacher, he had worked for the civil service. There was a shortage of Physics teachers at the time, and, as he had a Chemical Physics degree, Dan applied for and was accepted on a PGCE[3] programme to do Chemistry and Physics. He did his two main teaching practice placements in very deprived areas, where, Dan recalls, approximately 75% of the children were very under-developed and clinically ill. He explained that, throughout his career, he had always made positive choices to work in challenging schools, because he wanted to 'make a difference'. He came into teaching in the first place because he enjoys working with young people. He reflected that he was still very positive about his job as a classroom teacher.

When he qualified as a teacher, Dan applied for and was appointed to the teaching pool of a large, urban LEA. He accepted a post soon after in what he described as 'an ordinary school', although he recalled that it was a 'funny place'. He stayed there for two years, during which time he developed an interest in pastoral care. Wanting to take on more pastoral responsibility, he became a head of year[4] in his next school, a position he held for five years before moving on again, this time to take up a role as key stage 4 science leader. He moved again after a year, to take on a role as key stage 3 co-ordinator, a post he held for 18 months. He then moved to a post as head of science in a school he described as 'the worst school in Britain', with only 1% of pupils gaining grades A–C[5] at GCSE level. His next move was to a school in a different town, as faculty team leader in science.

Subsequently, he was promoted to the role of super-faculty team leader in another school. At this point, he started to encounter some difficulties. He related how he experienced a serious crisis of confidence, which disrupted his life and career somewhat: 'After that I left. No job to go to. I had a bit of a blip'. He started work as a supply teacher in a new school, and was appointed head of science after three months. At the time of the interview, he had been at that same school for 11 years, and had also taken on the role of Initial Teacher Training (ITT) co-ordinator.

One of the key changes Dan said he had seen during his career was the expectation in recent years that there would be support in place for new teachers in schools. This, he said, was very different from his own experiences as a novice in the late 1980s, when he did not have any support from a mentor. In his role as ITT co-ordinator, he was keenly aware of the need to support and nurture early career teachers. He considered this support to be even more important as teacher recruitment had become increasingly challenging. He reflected that ever higher expectations and an excessive workload discouraged people from teaching, or led them to leave within a couple of years of qualifying. For Dan, workload was one of the most negative aspects of the job.

Dan talked in detail about the impact of a succession of policies on schooling, children and his work as a teacher. He talked too about how important it had been to him that there had been increasing emphasis on equal opportunities in education during the course of his teaching career. As a gay man, he explained that this shift affected him deeply:

When I started teaching in [place] it was still a crime [to be gay] [...] I've been through section twenty-eight[6] [...] the whole works. And actually, for the first time, this year [...] we had posters up [in school] for LGBT, for the first time in my entire teaching career. It's a big change.

Dan explained that he had had to switch roles in the last few years, which had entailed accepting a cut in salary. He said that he was too 'scared' to apply for posts elsewhere, feeling that he had become 'institutionalised', and that his experience had been 'devalued'. He commented, 'when I hit fifty, I thought, that's it. No-one else will want me [...] Fifty-year-olds, we're seen as

has-beens in this school [...] There are very few fifty-year olds left'.
At 53 years, he told me, he was the oldest teacher in the school.
He was planning to retire at 60 years.

EDNA: 'PLODDING ON'

At the time of the interview, Edna was planning to retire. The love
of her subject, history, had brought her into the teaching profession
in the first place, although she, like others, recalled that in the early
to mid-1970s she had had very few career options: 'I wanted to do
something with history and what can you do with history apart
from teaching?' She added that she received very little guidance at
school, and that she never had a career plan. Looking back, she said
she thought perhaps she had been 'a bit naïve'.

Edna went to college to train as a teacher, starting a three-year
degree course in 1973. There were very few jobs available by the
time she had completed the course, but she managed to find a post
in her home town, where she then stayed for three years. When she
married, her husband was unable to find work in the same town,
and had to accept a position in another city. Edna was unable to
find a teaching job in the city, and so she accepted a post in the civil
service, where she worked for five years.

Edna and her husband started a family. When her children
started school, Edna started going into their schools as a helper.
She recalled that her colleagues in her children's schools encouraged
her to return to teaching. She applied for a 'return to teaching'
programme and was accepted, starting her course in 1990.
She explained that she was fortunate because she learned on the
course about the National Curriculum, which put her in a stronger
position to find a post. On her return to teaching, she worked
initially as a supply teacher. After 6 months of supply teaching,
she was offered a three-day per week post, and eventually a
full-time position, at the same school, which she accepted gladly.

Returning to teaching after the break in her career, Edna saw
a significant change in the culture and practices of education.
She recalled that before her break, it had been much more relaxed.
Teachers had had, she recalled, the flexibility to teach to their strengths,
and to adapt what they were doing in accordance with what they

and the children felt like doing. She and her colleagues had made the most of their professional freedom to set up library vans and take children to listen to writers speaking, to enthuse pupils about reading. Edna regretted that this sort of initiative could not happen now.

Edna's experience of the impact of a succession of reforms had been mixed. In the uncertainty of the ever-shifting policy context, she had felt 'a bit lost' and in need of leadership at various points in her career. At the same time, she saw that there had been benefits as well as challenges. She had a positive view of the National Curriculum, seeing that it provided a useful structure for the curriculum, even if some of it had been difficult to implement. She saw, too, that there was now a lot more support for Newly Qualified Teachers (NQTs) and student teachers. Like Dan, she had received very little guidance herself when she was a novice teacher.

She was very appreciative of the friendship and support of colleagues in the school, whom she described in the most positive of terms. She had very much appreciated being able to team teach and identified this collaborative approach to working as key, encouraging her to keep 'plodding on' rather than retiring early.

FREDA: 'CHANGE IS PREFERABLE TO STAGNATION'

Freda had recently retired at the time of the interview, although she was still doing some work with trainee teachers and what she termed 'struggling teachers'. She had started teaching in 1977. Her interest in her subject had led her to choose secondary school teaching as a career in the first place. She taught for eight years in a school in a large city, during which time she progressed to acting head of department and then head of year. She got married, took two maternity leaves and moved to a different area of the country, where her husband, also a teacher, had secured a post in a new school. Freda found a job in the same school as her husband, and she stayed there for 19 years, until her retirement.

At the start of her career, Freda had aspired to become a headteacher. When she had children, however, she re-assessed this aspiration. She commented,

You accept that once you've got children, things are not necessarily as straightforward. Once you've got two people, particularly two people in teaching, one career sometimes has to give.

We decided, I don't know quite why, that my husband had better career prospects, being a scientist. That's very sexist isn't it?

Looking back over her teaching career, Freda reflected that the impact of policy change on her work as a teacher had been 'huge'. She described a time in the 1980s when 'everybody just did their own thing'. Teachers' aspirations for most of their pupils were low. There was very little in terms of lesson observation and training for novice teachers, and no real control over what teachers chose to do in the classroom.

Like Edna, Freda saw that the 'much more relaxed' culture of schooling that characterised the earlier years of her career changed from 1988 onwards. Successive reforms led to increased workload for teachers, exacerbated by shortage of funding. The early versions of the National Curriculum were too cumbersome, and the levels of attainment identified were not effective in ascertaining learning. Moreover, the highly prescriptive nature of the National Curriculum created practical challenges for schools and teachers, especially in the early days.

Increased accountability post-1988, in tandem with increased use of technology to track students' progress, meant much closer monitoring and control than at the start of Freda's career. With increased accountability, Freda observed, came a shifting of the responsibility for students' achievements from pupils to teachers and schools. This shift in turn effected a change in teachers' expectations of their pupils, moving towards what Freda termed an 'aspirational curriculum'. Higher expectations and aspirations led to developments in pedagogical practices.

Although having to deal with the impact of the many changes since 1988 had been destabilising and demoralising at times, Freda acknowledged the benefits of the National Curriculum, and felt on balance that change was preferable to stagnation.

GAIL: 'EXHAUSTED'

Gail started teaching in 1975, having completed her training for the Certificate in Education in the East Midlands. After a teaching pool interview, she was assigned to a local primary school, where she taught until 1982. During her time at the school, she took on responsibility for extracurricular activities, working evenings and weekends. This led eventually to her promotion to a scale 2 post.

In 1982, she became pregnant with her first child, and took a two-year career break. She had a second child five years later, and a third two years after that. She then returned to teaching on a part-time and supply basis, working in a range of schools. She estimated that during the 15 years she spent raising her family, she taught for around four years in total. Having raised her children, she was appointed to a temporary post in a local school. The post later became a permanent position. She took on the role of the school SENCo,[7] as well as that of maths and science co-ordinator. Looking back, she reflected that she had been somewhat overloaded with responsibilities by her headteacher at the time. She took a pay cut in order to move from the school to the school at which she was employed at the time of the interview. This was a primary school and academy, within a MAT. She recalled,

I moved here on a temporary contract, but as it happened it worked out and I became a SENCo here in about 2000, and I've been here ever since. Currently, I'm the modern foreign languages coordinator, and special needs coordinator and [...] one of the safeguarding team.

Like Freda, Gail was conscious that the culture of education and the work of teachers had changed considerably since her early years in the job. In particular, she recalled the freedom she had had earlier in her career to make her own decisions about what to teach, without feeling she was being 'watched'. She did, though, welcome the increased accountability that characterised the post-1988 era, and felt it had been needed. At the same time, she explained that she had found the pace of change in education to be 'relentless'. She felt she had survived the pressure by making up her own mind about what to teach and how. She was conscious of having decided for herself the changes she would implement and the pedagogical practices she would continue.

At the time of the interview, Gail's school, deemed by Ofsted to 'require improvement', was awaiting the next Ofsted inspection to ascertain whether 'improvement' had been achieved. Gail was feeling the pressure this entailed, describing her work as 'very full on', and herself as 'exhausted' and 'hopelessly behind'.

Gail reflected that her career as a teacher had not worked out the way she had expected it to be, for a variety of reasons. Some were personal, and connected with her role as a wife and mother. Others were connected with the way teaching had changed.

*She noted that there had been a shift in the expectations of teachers
and parents, which she placed in a context of wider societal change.*

HENRY: 'A JOB I THOUGHT I COULD DO'

*Henry had recently retired when the interview took place.
He recounted how he had become a teacher in the first place
because, 'it was a job I thought I could do […] It was about
the kids and giving them the opportunities that they deserved'.
He started out as a teacher of geography and history in 1981, in an
11–16 school in the East of England. He stayed there for 10 years,
becoming a head of department and head of year. He left the school
in 1991 to take up a post at another school as head of humanities,
a position he held for about six years. During this time, he was
seconded to the school senior leadership team (SLT) as senior
teacher, remaining on the SLT from 1998 to 2010. His main
responsibility was for mentoring trainee teachers. Henry was by this
time in his early fifties. He enjoyed the work he did with trainees,
but found the SLT work stressful and challenging.*

*Henry's school became an academy in 2010. When a new
headteacher was appointed, Henry negotiated with her and agreed
that he would step down from the SLT, if he could be given some
non-teaching time. She agreed, and in his final year of teaching,
Henry returned to the post of head of geography, before retiring
from the profession after a 34-year career. He explained that he had
wanted to enjoy the last couple of years of his teaching career and
wanted to retire whilst he was still doing a good job.*

*Like other teachers in the study, Henry recalled that at the
start of his career, he had enjoyed the professional freedom to
make decisions about what to teach and how, but that the culture
had changed by the time he retired. He now felt that the pace of
change was constantly increasing, putting more and more pressure
on teachers. Describing teaching as 'a young person's game', he
expressed concern that the profession would lose experienced
teachers well ahead of retirement age as the job had become
unsustainable.*

*He identified a number of key changes he considered to have
been particularly significant during his career. These included the
introduction of the GCSE, which he saw as a positive step forward,*

*and the National Curriculum levels of attainment, which were
rather less helpful. The introduction of Ofsted had significantly
impacted schools' and teachers' work. In addition, the increasing
prevalence of ICT in schools, and the increased responsibility
teachers now had for safeguarding children, had meant that the job
was very different from Henry's work at the start of his career.*

*Teamwork and good working relationships with his colleagues
had been very important features of his day-to-day working life,
sustaining him and enabling the schools in which he worked to
be successful.*

IRENE: 'I DON'T THINK CHOICE IS WHAT DELIVERS QUALITY'

*Irene was 58 years old and about a month away from retirement
at the time of the interview. She had started teaching in 1981,
initially at a large community college in the Midlands. She taught
sociology and humanities in the school for 21 years, during which
time she was gradually promoted until she became head of the
humanities faculty.*

*When she became a mother, Irene decided to step down from
her curricular responsibility. She accepted a pay cut, and returned
to a standard teaching post. In 2002, she was appointed to a post
as a teacher of sociology in a sixth form college,[8] where she was
still working when I interviewed her. She commented that the
college was 'delightful' compared to her previous school, which she
had been finding increasingly difficult. She had taught a range of
subjects in the college, including sociology, health and social care,
politics and citizenship. She held leadership responsibilities as she
had become head of citizenship and assistant curriculum leader. Her
leadership responsibilities included taking charge of two subjects
and supervision of other teachers.*

*Like Henry, Irene was clear that technology had significantly
changed teachers' work and impacted on their daily, working lives.
Whilst technology had, in her view, improved teaching and learning,
it had also meant teachers had to work harder.*

*Looking back over her career, Irene commented that she had
never anticipated that there would have been so much change,
or that education would become 'such a political football'.
She reflected on how constant change had become the norm*

for teachers. Whilst there had been, Irene felt, some positive improvements, she found some of the impacts of policy to be quite abhorrent, and counter to her values. She observed that schools had become 'less and less' about 'genuinely caring for students'. The culture had re-configured such that:

[There] is extra work, extra surveillance of what teachers are doing, and competition between teachers, even within schools. Neoliberalism has been extended into the schools, with competitions for the best teacher award and things like that.

Interestingly, the policy Irene said she most regretted overall was the dismantling of the LEAs:

I would change the policy that took away the control of education by local government. I don't understand the thinking behind free schools[9] and academies and there is no democratic accountability in that. I don't think choice is what delivers quality.

Irene still loved teaching and working with students. She was also clear, though, that she was glad her career was nearly over, as she did not feel optimistic about the future of schooling in England.

I have provided in this chapter a short introduction to and vignette of each of the nine participants in the study. In Chapter 6, I draw on all nine testimonies to present the teachers' perceptions of the impact of policy shift on their work.

NOTES

1. In the early 1980s, the teachers' pay structure was such that new teachers would begin as Scale 1 teachers and could apply for and obtain promotions during their career to progress to Scale 2, Scale 3, Scale 4 and Scale 5 posts. A Scale 2 post was typically a first post of responsibility, such as assistant head of department.

2. The National Strategies (1997–2011) were intended to raise standards and improve the teaching of core subjects. They included the National Literacy Strategy, the National Numeracy Strategy, the Key Stage 3 Strategy and the Early Years Foundation Stage. The National Strategies were extended to all core subjects, to Key Stage 4 as well as Key Stage 3, and to Early Years, Behaviour and Attendance, the School Improvement Partner programme and Special Educational Needs (see DfE, 2011).

3. PGCE – Postgraduate/Professional Certificate in Education – the main teaching qualification in the UK.

4. Head of Year – a middle leadership post with responsibility for pastoral care of a cohort of students and the leadership of a team of tutors.

5. At the time of the interview, the GCSE examination was graded A–G. Grades A–C were considered equivalent to the former 'O' levels, reflecting the achievements of more able students and so used in ascertaining the 'effectiveness' of schools and their position in league tables.

6. Section 28 was the section of the Local Government Act of 1988 that prohibited the promotion of homosexuality in schools. It was repealed in 2003.

7. SENCo – Special Educational Needs Co-ordinator.

8. Sixth form college – a college for 16–19 year olds offering academic qualifications such as 'A' levels and GCSEs as well as a range of other options.

9. Free Schools – Free schools can be set up by a range of groups such as charities, parents, universities, businesses, etc. They do not have to provide the National Curriculum and can make their own decisions about staffing, term times and so forth.

Chapter 6

FINDINGS AND DISCUSSION (I): PERCEPTIONS OF THE IMPACT OF POLICY SHIFT SINCE 1988 ON TEACHERS' WORK

INTRODUCTION

Although each interview elicited a unique story, it was possible to identify four common, cross-sample themes related to the impact of educational policy since 1988 on the teachers' work. Resonating with the literature reviewed in Chapters 1 and 2, participants' insights indicate that radical changes in the culture and working practices of schools have taken place over the period of their careers. Policy shift since 1988 was seen to have led to:

- increased prescription, accountability and an erosion of teachers' freedom;

- longer working hours, increased workload and pressure on teachers;

- changes in the culture of schooling and the nature of teaching; and

- increased challenges resulting from the changes.

The findings are presented in this chapter under the above four thematic headings. I identify cross-sample commonalities where these were apparent in the teachers' testimonies, whilst also showing that there was divergence in the detail of their discussions. Pseudonyms are used throughout.

INCREASED PRESCRIPTION, ACCOUNTABILITY
AND AN EROSION OF TEACHERS' FREEDOM

All participants reported that there had been a gradual erosion of their freedom over the course of their careers, with 1988 being a significant turning point. The ERA (1988), they reflected, had led to reduced scope to make decisions and choices in their day-to-day work post-1988, as schooling had become increasingly characterised by a culture of prescription and accountability. Participants reported experiencing increased control from external sources over their work, and constraints on their freedom to choose what to teach, and how. The introduction of the National Curriculum and its associated focus on assessment was perceived to have had significant impact (see Fielding, 2006; Stevenson & Wood, 2013).

The teachers linked the constraints they had experienced to the development of an extensive set of accountability measures, and the intensification of accountability structures and processes (see Green, 2011). Ofsted was perceived to be a national agency for enforcing change (see Baxter, 2013; Baxter et al., 2015), driving the strong national and institutional emphasis on assessment, measurable outcomes and testing that now defined the nature of teachers' work (see Fielding, 2006; Stevenson & Wood, 2013).

The teachers viewed the constraints they described as characteristic of a culture in which they were not trusted. In contrast, they recalled feelings of being trusted pre-1988, when they had had the freedom to decide both what and how they would teach. Then, they recalled, they could use their judgement to make curricular and pedagogical decisions in accordance with what they understood to be the needs of their pupils. I cite illustrative examples of this set of perceptions below.

Both Barbara and Anna had started teaching in 1977, more than a decade before the introduction of the National Curriculum. This was a time when, Anna recalled, teachers could plan for themselves what they would cover in the curriculum, and how. As Barbara commented, 'you didn't really give any planning in, and nobody really knew what you were teaching'. Similarly, Edna, who had qualified in 1976, recalled that when she started, there was greater flexibility and freedom for teachers:

> In those days you could go more with what the children wanted to do [...] It was a much easier, laid-back atmosphere [...] You could teach to your strengths, what you felt like doing more. (Edna, primary school teacher)

Reflecting that teachers were now much more accountable, Anna regretted the erosion of her autonomy in the classroom:

> *You've got to have the freedom to teach your way [...] If you want to instill the passion, and love, of language and literature in children and young people, the curriculum can't be too rigid. I know there's a school of thought that it has to be, and there are certain things you do have to do, but you still need to have that flair, to be able to react to things [...], because, you're impassioned about things, but you've got to get [the children] to be as well [...] So, you have to have that freedom to be able to adapt, I think, in an English curriculum. I'm not at all sure that senior management [...] agree with that. But [...] you can't just [say], 'Oh, its October the fifth, we're all doing this', because English isn't like that. (Anna, primary school teacher and English and literacy coordinator)*

Professionalism and self-belief were seen to be diminished as a result of the increased emphasis since 1988 on assessment, testing and measurable progress. Dan, for instance, reflected:

> *[The over-emphasis on measurement and testing] has led to teachers' professionalism being undermined in a big way. I used to be able to say, 'that student is not a level five', meaning, at that moment, with fairly good confidence that they would make progress. But now they've got to make X amount of progress, but a lot of the time [the progress] doesn't happen, and you're left feeling a lack of confidence in yourself [...] and lack of confidence in the data [...] Some kids never come to school, but we still have targets to set [...] and [...] you have to keep records of what you have done: 'I 'phoned home on this day. I sent a letter home on this day. I spoke to them on this day'. You have to keep a spreadsheet of that! [...] Teaching is no longer seen as a profession. We are no longer seen as autonomous. We are now, I don't know, puppets almost. (Dan, secondary school teacher)*

In Dan's view, this gradual de-professionalisation of teachers was quite detrimental, leading to frustration, erosion of self-belief and ultimately de-motivation. He explained:

> *It's still in my heart. I make a difference, but I also know that against some measures that difference is not being measured.*

*And that's quite hard, and I find myself being angry all the time
about things I can't change. That's really frustrating, because you
come in and you think, 'Well, I know I am making a difference', but
against some measures I'm not making a difference, and it's really
hard to have that belief in yourself. (Dan, secondary school teacher)*

The teachers' testimonies suggested that, since 1988, teachers' judgement had diminished in importance, having been replaced by quantitative data and attainment target regimes. 'Progress' was now understood through the narrow medium of numeric data. There was greater emphasis on testing, both internal and external, and continual monitoring of measurable progress to ensure that children were meeting targets. Teachers' work was placed under permanent scrutiny. In some cases, senior leaders in schools had introduced structures requiring regular input of statistical data, with a constant focus on assessment. Consonant with Fielding's (2006, p. 364) analysis, emphasis was being placed, on 'precision of targets and delivery'. The imperative to monitor and demonstrate pupil progress meant that teachers' work had become more uniform and more intense (see Valli & Buese, 2007), with more of their time having to be spent on activities not directly related to teaching, such as tracking pupils and analysing data. For primary school teacher Gail, Ofsted-led priorities had been very influential in the development of an intensely data-driven culture in her school:

*It is a lot of paperwork and data heavy [...] It's all for Ofsted,
because Ofsted say, if these children are making good progress,
give me the evidence. So, it is all driven by that, and professional
judgement isn't evidence. So, we are very paperwork-heavy
and everything has to be done within a timescale. (Gail, primary
school teacher)*

Increased accountability and a strong emphasis on assessment and measurable progress had inevitably led to longer working hours, greater pressure and a heavier workload for teachers, as I discuss below.

LONGER WORKING HOURS, INCREASED WORKLOAD AND PRESSURE ON TEACHERS

All participants talked about the increased workload, pressure and long hours that had come to characterise the daily reality of their work, echoing the findings of Day and Smetham (2009) and Valli and Buese (2007). In accounting for how this change had come about, the teachers made reference to key policy shifts, notably the introduction of Ofsted, the National Curriculum and levels of attainment. Interestingly, the participants did not, for the most part, reject the policies *per se*; in most cases they conceded that the policies had been well intentioned. Problems were perceived to have resulted not from the essence of the policies, but from the ways in which they had been devised and implemented nationally. There was a perceived disconnect between policymakers and the work of schools and classroom teachers. Those devising policy reforms were seen to lack understanding of the day-to-day working reality of schools. Policymakers' lack of understanding was seen by the teachers to result in the issuing of imperatives that were unworkable, and that resulted in unmanageable levels of bureaucracy.

There was concern, too, about the pressure associated with the *pace* of change (see Wood, 2019), exacerbated, participants explained, by the need to be permanently ready for Ofsted inspection. An excessive workload resulted, viewed by some participants as the root cause of problems with teacher recruitment and retention. I include below some quotes from participants to provide a flavour of the kind of workload-related reflections harnessed in the interviews.

The National Curriculum was discussed at length in all nine interviews. Concerns about the associated increased workload were expressed in terms of the unwieldy and unmanageable bureaucratic burden that the National Curriculum implementation had entailed in its various stages. It is noteworthy that there was not a strong, overall sense of antipathy to the underpinning philosophy of the notion of a National Curriculum. Secondary school teacher Cathy, for example, who described the introduction of the National Curriculum and levels of attainment as 'death by ring binder', explained:

> *Everything was stepped and measured and levelled. The idea was good, but the minute detail and the bureaucracy connected with it was soul destroying for teachers. All these things have the kernel of really good practice, but you could tell that [...] people in offices somewhere had added more and added more and added more. So, that policies were made [...] without a real understanding of practical, day-to-day, what it's like to be in a busy school, where [...] people are fully timetabled to deliver and there isn't [...] the luxury of time for marking and preparation. When you're talking about personalization, individual learning plans for kids, that's very, very time consuming, as well. That was never really taken on board [...] The bureaucracy was really burdensome. The ideas themselves were good. (Cathy, secondary school teacher)*

Similarly, secondary school teacher Freda acknowledged the benefits of a National Curriculum, whilst also recalling that its prescriptive nature had created practical difficulties for schools and teachers, especially in the early days. Like others, she commented that the early versions of the National Curriculum were cumbersome and over-detailed, yet not fit for purpose in terms of ascertaining learning:

> *The first National Curriculum was unworkable for several of the subjects. So, for instance, for geography – the key stage three curriculum was announced and there were 103 things we had to test kids against. I think it actually was 103 things we had to teach kids and test kids against [...] It was a very, very difficult thing, because, for instance, with geography, they levelled knowledge: 'If you know this, that's that level. If you know this, that's that level'. Well, some kids with a very good memory [...] could get a higher level because they knew the capitals of twenty-eight places [...] So, it was very difficult to level kids. (Freda, secondary school teacher)*

Constant monitoring and assessment of pupils featured prominently in participants' accounts of how and why workload and pressure had increased (see Day & Smethem, 2009). Commenting on this, secondary school teacher Dan explained that he saw the heavy workload as the main reason why schools were struggling to recruit and retain new teachers:

> *I think the expectations are much higher. I think the workload is incredibly high. I'm not sure I could do it nowadays. Start again. I mean, obviously, I am a teacher and I am doing it. But, I'm not sure if I could find my feet these days [...] Workload is the main issue – all the futile attempts to balance that work quota. It's absolutely incredible when you see some of these young teachers, who don't know how to take shortcuts, killing themselves. That's the bit that worries me, looking on. And that's the bit that, I think, is why people are leaving. They're just not prepared. I don't think they're prepared for just how intense it is [...] The workload is still increasing [as a result of the] pointless marking and the continual, futile assessment, the going back and assessing those that have missed the assessment and all that kind of thing, and the looped assessment. Having to show pupils made improvement one assessment to the next. The expectation that there is a linear progression, which, you know, there is not a linear progression. All students progress at different rates, but they're all measured against the same baselines. So, they're all expected to make two levels [of progress], or one flight path, or however it's measured. (Dan, secondary school teacher)*

Linked to the assessment culture, Ofsted emerges as a significant and enduring source of anxiety. The introduction of Ofsted was deemed to have had the greatest impact on teachers' work. Ofsted inspectors 'visit'. They are not present all the time. Yet, the need to be Ofsted-ready is a constant pressure. Many of the participants highlighted the volume of work which they believed needed to be completed to maintain school systems which were permanently 'Ofsted ready', and which increased to new levels of intensity when it was known that Ofsted would visit.

Primary school teacher Gail's school had just come out of special measures at the time of the interview and was now in the 'requires improvement' category. This entailed sustained pressure on the school and its teachers, which Gail was experiencing acutely:

> *The work is very full on. I still teach full time and I'm exhausted.*
> *The requirements are just ridiculous and [...] we're expecting*
> *Ofsted at any point [...] There are not enough hours in the day to*
> *do all the marking, because [senior leaders] are monitoring again.*
> *When I go home at night, I'm exhausted, and then I have to start*
> *again. I have to get up at five to plan the day, or I work until two*
> *in the morning to plan the next day. I don't work on Saturday at all*
> *unless I have to, but on Sunday, from midday until late at night, I'm*
> *working. (Gail, primary school teacher)*

Participants were concerned not only about the increased workload resulting from policy shifts, but also about the detrimental impact of the accelerated *pace* of change, especially on newer teachers' potential longevity in the profession:

> *Personally, I think that change is coming faster and faster, and*
> *there are more and more demands being put on people. I was*
> *looking at my colleagues who I taught with, who were young with*
> *smiley faces, and I was thinking 'You won't be able to sustain this*
> *in five years' time, and you're only twenty-five; in five years' time*
> *I don't think you'll be doing this job because you are working*
> *every hour of the day' [...] I think that teaching today is a young*
> *person's game and if we are not careful in another ten years' time*
> *all the experienced teachers will have gone. So, you are talking*
> *about teachers at the age of forty thinking that they can't do this*
> *anymore. That is worrying me about education and about them*
> *as individuals, because I can't see how they can sustain that. I*
> *worked with two absolutely cracking teachers last year. They were*
> *brilliant and really keen, but you're thinking 'You're here till sixty;*
> *I'm not sure you can do that'. (Henry, secondary school teacher)*

As well as the impact on workload, and the implications for recruitment and retention of teachers, increased accountability and prescription were perceived to have entailed shifts in the culture of schooling and the work of teachers, as I explore below.

CHANGES IN THE CULTURE OF SCHOOLING
AND THE NATURE OF TEACHERS' WORK

All participants saw that a succession of policy shifts had effected changes in the culture of schooling, and so in the nature of teachers' work. Their perceptions of this change in culture were multifaceted and complex. There were, though, certain discernible themes in the teachers' accounts of their career experiences. First, teachers had become more accountable within a culture in which consumers (parents and children) had a sense of entitlement to a service. Second, the introduction of standardised tests in tandem with the use of technology to track and monitor pupil progress had led to higher expectations in terms of pupil outcomes. Third, teachers were now playing a much larger pastoral and caring role in terms of safeguarding and socialising children. I present below extracts from the teacher narratives that illustrate these themes.

Freda, who had started teaching in 1977, noted that over the years, teachers and schools had come to be held more accountable for students' achievements:

> In the past, the students were responsible for the results that they
> got, rather than the teacher, and certainly not the school. The school
> wasn't responsible for results. The kids were responsible for the
> results. (Freda, secondary school teacher)

As teacher and school accountability had started to increase post-1988, Freda noted that a sense of entitlement began to emerge, as parents also became much more demanding:

> Parents could find out what the National Curriculum was, and
> they knew what kids were supposed to be being taught, and they
> knew what the levels were. And [...] if you were at all vague at
> parents' evening, some of them would come along with chapter
> and verse and a table quoting what was what, and they would
> question [...] We've had parents' evenings when parents come with
> all the evidence. That has been a very big change [...] Some of
> the parents are very clued up. I have to say almost all parents are
> very supportive of whatever school their student is in, unless there

have been specific problems, but they can also be very demanding, because, they feel that they are entitled to a service now [...] and they feel that they have the right, if you like, to question what's going on. Fair enough. You know? It's your child's future isn't it? But, yeah. Things have changed hugely [...] So, I think [teachers] had to get much more on the ball. (Freda, secondary school teacher)

Moreover, the pressure to monitor progress against levels of attainment had been intensified through the ubiquitous application of technology:

The world has changed because of computers [...] You can now track what your kids are doing, compared to what they did in primary school. Before the National Curriculum you couldn't track [...] what they had done at key stage three, let's say, before there was any kind of standardised testing [...] They do standardised testing of all kinds now, and so, you can work out where they should be, where they are and so on [...] It's a huge difference. Pupils are aware of what their targets are [...], and then what their aspirational targets are, what their minimal targets are, what they have to do to do this. They have a huge amount of information. For teachers you can identify immediately where the problems are. Which groups [...], which students are not on track, and nobody should fall through the crack. (Freda, secondary school teacher)

Freda reflected that this was a more responsible way of teaching, monitoring and tracking students than what she saw as the more *laissez-faire* culture of her earlier years in the profession. She went on to discuss how the increased accountability of schools and teachers had led to changes in terms of teachers' higher expectations of their pupils:

[During my earlier teaching years], for the clever students, which was a small proportion, there was the aspiration that they would [...] go on to do something in terms of career. People didn't have to go to university in those days, but we hoped that a lot of them would go on to further education of some sort. But, for the vast majority of the kids, there was no such aspiration, really. It was OK. They could do quite well and go on and get a job and that was it. And it was a very different [...] set up. Only about a quarter of the students were expected to do O-Levels, never mind A[1]-Levels [...] They were aimed at the top twenty-five percent of the ability range in schools, I think. And certainly, the rest of them did CSEs. And huge numbers of kids got grade four CSE, which really was a

*very low-grade qualification. Looking back on it now, it really was
not worth much [...] but, nobody else outside the school cared.
There was no accountability for schools. Even the borough weren't
bothered about results. (Freda, secondary school teacher)*

Whereas Freda recognised that there were some positive benefits to tracking and monitoring pupils, others viewed the overemphasis on measurement
and tests as detrimental to learning and motivation:

*It seems we're just working to tests now and looking at data.
The last three or four years have been so much about data [...] I
feel very sorry for the children. The bad behaviour we're getting
in Year Six is because we've been pumping them for six, seven,
eight months, but now they're just playing up. They're used to the
structure of, 'Right, we do a SATS test. We go through it'. [...] It's
so boring! The kids get bored [...] it's a sad state. (Edna, primary
school teacher)*

Unlike Edna, most participants did not make explicit links between the
testing culture and declining pupil behaviour. However, it was interesting that
some discussed how their role had increasingly involved safeguarding and
socialising children in ways that went beyond the sort of pastoral care in
which they were engaged earlier in their careers. Comments included:

*It was once just purely teaching. You taught the children and you had
fun with them, and if it was a nice day, you went out to do rounders,
or to collect berries for the nature table. It was just much more
relaxed [...] but now it's become a thing where we teach them their
manners, and we stop them getting into gangs; we do the social work
side; we do safeguarding; we have got to cover gun crime and street
crime. Every ill in society is now the teacher's role. Everything is done
in school [...] It is almost like parents appear to have defaulted on
their role and it's been pushed into the schools by the government. I
mean the safeguarding thing is huge, and we are covering FGM² – the
list is huge. I do understand that we see the children every day and
I think safeguarding is necessary, but that is a reflection on what is
happening in society, surely. (Gail, primary school teacher)*

*[There have been changes in terms of] things like safeguards and
stuff like that, and although we were all responsible for the students
we taught back in the early '80s, we didn't think about anything
like that. That doesn't mean to say that you didn't take precautions,
and that you weren't aware of things, and if you had a child coming*

*into school upset, you wanted to find out what was wrong with
them, if they allowed you. But now we seem to have more and
more onus being put on teachers […] So, I think there is more
overt responsibility put on teachers now than there was when I first
started. (Henry, secondary school teacher)*

Participants' experiences and perceptions of changes in the culture of
schooling and the nature of teachers' work varied. There was, however, consensus that change had entailed challenge for teachers, as I discuss in the next
section below.

INCREASED CHALLENGES RESULTING
FROM THE CHANGES

The policy changes that were deemed to have presented teachers the greatest challenges were identified as those pertaining to Ofsted and SATs. Whilst
the participants variously reported positive, negative and mixed experiences of
Ofsted, there was consensus that preparing for, undergoing and acting on the
outcomes of an Ofsted inspection presented significant challenges to schools
and teachers. The introduction and subsequent revisions to SATS were seen
to have been problematic, and to have had some detrimental effects on pupils
and teachers. I include here extracts from two teachers' narratives to portray
how they made sense of the challenges that had resulted from these two major
policy shifts.

*I think the big policy change wasn't for me National Curriculum
but Ofsted. I think that is the thing that has impacted on schools,
and this idea of having league tables. When I went to [name of
school], Ofsted was just coming online and, in those days, you
were given months [notice of inspection] I remember coming back
to school after Christmas in '93 or something like that and being
told that Ofsted are coming, but not until October. And, although
we really didn't know enough in those days about what an Ofsted
inspection looked like, we put a lot of effort into making sure that
we got it right. So, we had our first inspection and we were fine.
I think we were inspected two or three years later and it was much
the same sort of thing, but then slowly Ofsted began to change, and
its power and influence began to change, and when we introduced
league tables for schools, that was not the best thing for education
[…] [Ofsted] did say that it took the social and economic contexts
of the schools into consideration, but I don't think that is true.*

*I've been Ofsteded five or six times now [...] By [the time of my
last Ofsted] we didn't know when Ofsted were coming, so you were
constantly looking over your shoulder to make sure that this or that
was right. I'm not necessarily sure that that is a very healthy way to
work. I taught a class of about thirty kids and they were targeted
to get so many percentage of C, but you and I know that two or
three of them could have a bad day, and if that happened when the
exam comes, then those results could be really impacted upon by
just a handful of kids. That is where I've got this worry. Schools are
obviously trying to drive standards forward but there seems to be
this idea that progress has to come at any cost, and that isn't always
possible with all kids. So that is where I get a little bit concerned
about that policy. I suppose in my latter few years I've always
been thinking that I'm being asked to achieve something that
I actually don't think is attainable. I've found that quite frustrating.
(Henry, secondary school teacher)*

*The emphasis [in school] is on SATs. You always have to keep getting
better and better [...] [SATS have] caused us so many problems,
because we have no idea how to assess the children. We've tried
all sorts of methods, and it was a nightmare for the SEN children
because it seemed that they were making no progress whatsoever.
The kids were in such a state the last time we did SATs that we just
couldn't do it, because it was just too hard. The maths was not quite
where I would have liked it, but it wasn't too bad, but the reading
just overcame them [...] [The writing] was OK, because we are good
at writing here, and they did very well, but the reading was a huge
shock. I wasn't involved last year in the teaching of reading, but I
know how hard my colleague worked and she was just in bits when
the results came through. We thought we had done everything, but
the paper was much harder than we anticipated. I thought, with the
old SATs, we had got them pretty much worked out, but I think the
new SATs have been the last straw, with SPAG[3] and all the rest of it
[...] The new SPAG is ridiculous for children of this age; they do not
need to know the subjunctive and all that. I mean most adults on
the street wouldn't know what we were talking about. I think there
is too much detail in the new one. I thought the old SPAG was fine,
and the old writing was great, and we knew how to level the writing,
and the old paper was fine, but the new papers go beyond what is
necessary. (Gail, primary school teacher)*

Despite the challenges and their increased workload, the teachers did not necessarily oppose the changes in policy that had framed their work post-1988. Some were keen to point out that certain of the key policy shifts had brought benefits to children. Some of their comments were supportive of the evolving system, such as an appreciation of the need for a National Curriculum, which was seen as a positive development by some of the teachers. Those who were supportive of a national, agreed, curriculum believed that it led to a more coherent system, ensuring that children would be exposed to a structured experience. There was a general consensus on the importance of ensuring that all children are given the best opportunities to reach their potential. Participants agreed with the principle of inclusion and saw it as imperative that all children's needs should be identified and met. The emphasis on meeting the needs of all pupils contrasted with the past, the teachers suggested, when some children, particularly low-ability children, were ignored, depressing their aspirations and limiting their progression. Moreover, the teachers accepted and supported the values that underpinned the notion of accountability, if not the ways in which it had played out. Some reflected that the *laissez-faire* culture pre-1988 had not always been beneficial.

These concessions emerge, though, as relatively minor positives set against the more negative reflections on erosion of teacher freedom, and the potential for policies to be misapplied or lead to management regimes in school which are not conducive to teachers' work and development. In general, the changes the teachers described were seen in a negative light. Participants generally saw the implementation of the National Curriculum as badly handled and overbearing. The process had been over-bureaucratic and hyper-regulated, and was perceived as a threat to teachers' freedom, entailing considerable increases in workload. National Curriculum was also seen as linked to an increase in assessment, both internal and external, which in turn, also impacted on workload.

In sum, the insights gained from the teachers suggest that policy impinged on their work primarily through changes in curriculum, accountability, and Ofsted. The findings broadly confirm the literature reviewed in the early chapters of the book, and are perhaps unsurprising. Policy changes were for the most part perceived as having generally negative impacts, particularly on teachers' freedom and workload, and were therefore seen to have had a negative impact on the work of the career-long teachers.

Given this, why, and how, did they manage to stay in the profession? I turn in the next chapter to a consideration of what the career-long teachers identified to be the factors that helped sustain them long-term in the profession. I discuss the insights gathered into the ways in which the teachers had navigated policy over a sustained period of time and come to make their own decisions about how to mediate and implement change in their own classrooms

and schools. These insights shed new light on teachers' work, and their likelihood of longevity in the profession, in an era of change.

NOTES

1. Advanced levels, examinations taken at age 18.

2. Female genital mutilation.

3. Spelling and grammar.

Chapter 7

FINDINGS AND DISCUSSION (II): FACTORS HELPING TO SUSTAIN TEACHERS CAREER-LONG IN THE TEACHING PROFESSION

INTRODUCTION

As discussed in Chapter 6, the teachers' perceptions of the ways in which policy since 1988 had affected their daily work largely confirmed the findings of a range of other researchers, discussed in Chapters 1 and 2. The teachers' accounts of how and why they had managed to stay in the profession long-term were, however, enlightening and original. These findings offer new understandings of how this generation of teachers navigated the changes. They had found ways to stay in control of, and motivated in, their work.

The teachers' accounts reflected the sense they made of the combination of factors that had helped them to sustain their career-long commitment to teaching. It was possible to identify the following as key factors:

- The teachers' ability to take control of change.

- The teachers' appreciation of positive relationships in school.

- The teachers' sustained commitment to student success and making a difference.

- The teachers' concern to maintain a work–life balance.

Illustrated by extracts from the teachers' narratives, I present below the evidence suggesting that the factors above were central to their longevity in the profession.

TEACHERS' ABILITY TO TAKE CONTROL OF CHANGE

Taking control of the ways in which policy shifts were implemented in their own workplace seemed to be a key factor in teachers' ability to cope with the challenge of change. At the classroom level, taking control involved individual teachers in mediating and interpreting policy before making decisions about how it might be implemented in their teaching. At an institutional level, it involved school leaders or groups of teachers collaboratively mediating and implementing policy in ways that were suited to the context of their school and the children in it. I cite here brief extracts to illustrate participants' perspectives on this process as they had experienced it at the level of the classroom and the institution.

Primary school teacher Gail had found the pace of change to be 'relentless'. She explained that she had survived this pressure by, to an extent, making her own decisions about the changes she would implement, and the practices she would continue, in her own classroom. This is a theme running throughout Gail's narrative. She talked about the early days, when she made her own decisions in the absence of accountability, through to the post-1988 years, when she would both yield to prescription and make decisions for herself about what was effective:

> How I survived is, I have a core of things I think are good from the training that I get, and then I do what I feel is right [...] If I think something is not what I would do, then I won't always do it, if I can get away with it [...] I take what I think is a better idea and I will adapt my teaching to it. It is a lot of paperwork and data heavy and I just sometimes think 'Do I actually need to be doing all this?' Because I know what I'm doing [...] I could not go running around changing everything I do all the time [...] I do my job properly, and I do get good results, and my children make very good progress, and so [senior leaders] sort of leave me alone. My children don't make outstanding progress because we are fighting against a very deprived area, but they make good enough progress for me to show that I know what I'm doing. (Gail, primary school teacher)

Most participants reflected retrospectively on the need to mediate and interpret policy before institution-wide implementation, to ensure any changes introduced were adapted to suit their schools and their pupils. It seemed from the narratives that the teachers had gradually developed the confidence to do this over time, both individually and collectively. They used their judgement, even within a culture of increased prescription. They had not always had the confidence to do so. As Craft and Jeffrey (2008, p. 1) note, policy change from 1988 caused 'considerable stress' for teachers at the start. Secondary school teacher Anna, for example, recalled the panic that ensued following the release of the National Strategies, as teachers felt very unsure about what they were going to have to do. Reflecting back, Anna now felt that, instead of panicking, teachers needed to think through what would work in their particular context. She now realised she and her colleagues should 'just stay calm and pick out the bits that work for our school'. Primary school teacher Barbara made similar comments as she reflected on many years of implementing a succession of policy reforms. Experience had taught her that, although changes can seem daunting when they are first introduced, they tended to become more manageable, flexible and 'watered down' in the process of implementation.

Secondary school teacher Henry explained how he had had the confidence and self-belief to design a curriculum with which he was happy, rather than giving in to an 'obsession with levels' when National Curriculum and levels of attainment were introduced:

> When [National Curriculum] first started in the early '90s, we all had these folders for these levels, and these levels were split into attainment targets, and I think in geography we had thirty-two. People were going mad with these levels, and they were trying to make everything fit. So that they took their scheme of work and they said 'Where have we covered this? Where have we covered that?' And they were writing new schemes of work to try and fit it in, and each kid had a matrix with their name on it with all thirty-two levels across the top, and it was a tick box exercise! To me, I thought that this was not sustainable, because you can't keep doing it, and so I didn't bother. I just modelled the curriculum based on what I thought the National Curriculum was about. And our curriculum actually fitted very nicely with that, so I don't think that had a massive impact on us. So actually, with the National Curriculum, and the GCSE, for me, I think we could work with it. (Henry, secondary school teacher)

The insights gained from the teachers show that there were several factors which made their work sustainable. They identified mediating processes between policy and practice, at both the organisational and individual level. Some participants highlighted their willingness to choose the elements in new policy that they were willing to integrate into their practice. Where they could see the utility of a change, they would adopt it. Where they did not, they would tend to quietly ignore it. In addition, they were confident that if their results were good, they would tend to be 'left alone', and senior leaders would not focus intrusively on their practice. This suggests that for at least some, as their confidence had grown over time, they had felt increasingly at ease in mediating directives, confident in their 'professional mastery' (Chiong et al., 2017, p. 1083). Rather than complying passively with policy, or carrying out directives unquestioningly, they negotiated a strategy for implementation that was consistent with their values and commitment to students, grounded in their sustained experience and expertise. Their response to policy shift was more complex and nuanced than the buy-in or compliance described by Craft and Jeffrey (2008) or Ball (2003).

The teachers' perceptions of the nature of the changes in the culture and work of schools seemed to be linked to how they perceived their own capacity to act autonomously. In particular, the extent to which they perceived that they had the freedom to exert their agency in the classroom emerged as a key determining factor in how they viewed and enacted their daily work. The ways in which they engaged with reform seemed to be linked to their self-perceptions about their ability to take ownership and control of the change being made. This finding resonates with Kanter's (1983, p. 64) argument that change is 'exhilarating when it is done by us [and] considered positive when we are active contributors'. Longevity in the profession seems to be associated with the teachers' self-perceptions as 'active contributors' to change (Kanter, 1983, p. 64). If teachers see that there is scope to exert their professional agency, albeit within the constraints of reform imperatives, they are more likely to remain and take control of change. They are enabled to sustain their commitment and motivation when they see that there is some leeway to interpret, mediate and adapt reform to suit their schools and their students. These observations add to a body of literature that documents how teachers' personal dispositions (such as sense of vocation, motivation and self-efficacy) interplay with contextual support structures, for instance, in framing their resilience (see, e.g., Ainsworth & Oldfield, 2019; Boldrini et al., 2019; Day, 2008; Day & Hong, 2016; Gu, 2014), and so their likely longevity in the profession.

The self-perceptions of the teachers in this study were framed and influenced by the context in which they worked – including the children they taught, the colleagues with whom they collaborated and the school leaders, who set the tone and culture of the school. To sustain them in their work setting, they drew on their school teacher communities, often conceptualised as their professional 'families', for support, reinforcement and recognition at the local level. Their need to be a part of the school 'family' resonates with Gu's (2014) emphasis on the important role played by relationships in fostering resilience, commitment and motivation in teachers. The implication of this finding is that school leaders who are able to foster collegial, collaborative cultures in school are likely to be more conducive to ensuring continuity and retention of staff (see Day et al., 2007;

Ingersoll & Smith, 2003; Szczesiul & Huizenga, 2014). The teachers' collaboration and positive relationships with other colleagues undergirded the processes of mediation and implementation of policy, and were highly influential in helping to retain and sustain them in the teaching profession, as I discuss below.

TEACHERS' APPRECIATION OF POSITIVE RELATIONSHIPS IN SCHOOL

Participants were unanimous in stating the central importance of positive relationships in school as fundamental to their enjoyment of their daily work, their ability to cope with the pressure points and their scope to effect improvements. Positive relationships at all levels were highly valued: strong supportive leaders and line managers, closely-knit, collaborative teams, personal friendships and mutual support were all key factors, as I illustrate through selected quotes in this section.

At the macro-level, supportive and empowering line managers and senior leaders were viewed as fundamental in determining a high-quality experience of working life for participants. For example:

> I was very fortunate, because I started off my teaching career with a very supportive head of department, and I've worked with four heads, and they've always been very supportive with what I've tried to do. I've never felt unsupported in that context. (Henry, secondary school teacher)

At the meso-level, participants valued collaborative teamwork. For example:

> I like teamwork and I like being able to share ideas and take ideas from others. I like the sense of being in it together and supporting each other and recognizing the pressures on each other. (Irene, Sixth form college teacher)

> People come here, and they never want to leave, because we all work as a team. It's a huge staff, but there's no cliques. Whoever you work with, you just work with them. Over the last two years, we've gone to a team-teaching situation. So, in every classroom in our school, there are two people. In most of the classes, there are two teachers. So, I work with a young teacher, and we work as a team. She'll lead one thing and I will lead the other. And it is [...] really a good system. Before that we had smaller classes, but team-teaching situations are really good [...] We are well supported. (Barbara, primary school teacher)

*I've worked with dozens [of colleagues], and my last department
was a close-knit group [...] We had a new curriculum when we
became an academy and we worked together on it [...] and I've
always valued that [...] I think it's friendship, and it's teamwork,
and that is what I value [...] I think it is about teamwork, and
about respect. (Henry, secondary school teacher)*

Collaboration also took the form of professional dialogue, cited by a number of participants as very valuable for professional learning. For example:

*I used to love talking about education. I used to love talking about
what we were teaching, how we were teaching it, why we were
teaching it, who we were teaching it to and so on. And the best
CPD[1] days that we ever had were the ones where as departments,
we were together, when I ran the department, and we were talking
about how we could do things. I think most teachers go into
teaching, because they like teaching [...] I think most people are
passionate about getting the subject across, but mainly about giving
kids opportunities to learn stuff. I love talking education with
teachers. (Freda, secondary school teacher)*

Working closely with others in a culture of mutual support meant that teachers developed strong friendships and, in Anna's words, a sense of 'family'. There were many references to these supportive professional and personal relationships, for example:

*You can always find somebody to cry on their shoulder or to bolster
them. Most of us here are a very good team and will support each
other. I've got good colleagues who are friends and young teachers
as well and I'm not averse to saying to a young teacher 'that looks
really good; how do you do that?'. (Gail, primary school teacher)*

*People are very loyal to me. I've had, sort of, a family situation this
last month. And people in my department, younger teachers, have
said, 'Look, I will take that. I will mark that for you'. And they've
really rallied around me to get me through a difficult time with
family. [I value their] friendship. You've got to be able to talk to
each other and have a laugh. Because, it's not an easy job. If you
can't get on with the people you're working with, you make it even
more difficult. So, yeah... [I value their] loyalty and friendship. It's
the people that make a school [...] It's got to be the people in there
that make it a pleasant place to be [...] [so] they enjoy coming to
work. (Anna, secondary school teacher)*

Positive relationships in the workplace, therefore, emerged as a very important factor encouraging the teachers to remain in the profession long term. This finding resonates with George's (2009, p. 13) concept of the relational, psychological contract, in which emotional involvement figures highly. Collegiality was key to sustaining the teachers' engagement. Interviewees highlighted the role of collaborative work, which many saw as central to enjoyment and a feeling of achievement within the job. Some mentioned the sense of family they felt, reflecting the sense of 'personal identification with their organization' that George (2009, p. 13) highlights as characteristic of the relational contract. Strong institutional relationships supported the development of professional dialogue, which in turn offered the potential to unlock and sustain the teachers' freedom and autonomy.

The teachers' sense of belonging seemed to be conducive to the creation of shared values, to an extent echoing George's (2009) contention that employees with relational, psychological contracts internalise and identify with organisational values. That said, the values that underpinned the teachers' commitment to making a difference to their students seemed to be a stronger driver than affiliation with their employers' values *per se*, and echoing the findings reported by, for example, Kyriacou and Coulthard (2000) and Hobbs (2012), regarding teacher motivation. Whilst they were motivated by a sense of loyalty and belonging to their schools, their commitment to their students was the principal motivation. Underlying the teachers' espoused values was an authentic belief in the importance of helping young people achieve their potential, a commitment that was central to them staying within the profession. For some, this caring motivation extended to a sense of social justice woven into these relationships, as the teachers saw their role as being crucial in helping children from less advantaged backgrounds to improve their lives.

Positive relationships between colleagues were undergirded by a shared sense of values and a commitment to making a difference to students' lives. This appeared to be the primary motivator for teachers, and a strong driver encouraging them to stay in the profession, as I now discuss below.

TEACHERS' SUSTAINED COMMITMENT TO STUDENT SUCCESS AND MAKING A DIFFERENCE

A commitment to making a difference and seeing students succeed seemed to be fundamental to the teachers' motivation, and to the likelihood of their staying long term in the profession. The source of their motivation was evident in the way they talked about their love of classroom teaching, their liking for young people, and the satisfaction they derived from seeing students succeeding and improving their lives. Some examples follow.

> *I feel it's a privilege to be with young people [...] when you withdraw from them and have to do another job, you realize just how much you miss their energy and their take on life, and their humour. (Cathy, secondary school teacher)*

> *I really find [young people] inspirational and I get on with kids. I enjoy being with them, teaching them. (Dan, secondary school teacher)*

> *The best part of the job from my point of view is the students, and I love teaching politics. It's hard work, but it is really enriching. I've only been doing it for about four years but that has given me a real interest again [...] Teaching politics, there are wonderful activities to be involved in outside of the classroom, such as visiting parliament and that sort of thing. And being able to do that and working in a place that encourages that sort of thing and running a mock election or a referendum is so important. [I also appreciate] having good pastoral systems and, I would say, putting students first. (Irene, Sixth form college teacher)*

For secondary school teacher Henry, classroom teaching was the most important aspect of his work to him. He shared his recollections of a formative and affirming early career experience of teaching a particular group:

> *They were the nicest kids you could ever teach. So, it was things like that which made a big difference to me, because I looked forward to those Friday afternoons, because the kids were fantastic – they were keen and enthusiastic, and they enjoyed what they were doing – and once you've seen that, and that teaching can be like that, then there was no going back. And once the first set of results came out, we had a lot of success. It was from then on that we started to build, and you started to look forward to results day, and that was something that drove me on [...] Actually we shouldn't overlook that, because I don't care if you are a deputy head or an NQT, because ninety percent of what you do is actually in the classroom, so if you've got that right then you should be able to cope with the rest of it. Even when I was on the SLT, my teaching was always the most important thing. (Henry, secondary school teacher)*

The opportunity to work with young people attracted secondary school teacher Dan into teaching in the first place. Despite many frustrations resulting from the policy context and the shifting culture of schooling, Dan remained very positive about his job as a classroom teacher. He explained:

> *It's a really positive experience [...] When I'm in front of a bunch of kids, I can deliver and deliver quite well. I actually still love the teaching part of it. Even well, oh, it is twenty-eight years or something isn't it? Even after all this time, I still genuinely love the kids. Well, if you saw the cards I got at the end of term [....] They start to give you thank you cards and thank you cards that say, 'you were always there', or, 'you have made a difference', or whatever it is. I've always treasured those [...] They enjoy my lessons and I'm grateful [...] I still enjoy meeting students. I still enjoy listening to them, speaking to them. (Dan, secondary school teacher)*

Dan described how, throughout his career, he had made positive choices to work in challenging schools. He explained that he needed to feel he was 'making a difference', and that he derived great satisfaction from what he termed 'the success stories':

> *I've always treasured [...] it sounds corny saying 'watching them bloom', but there is something, when they see success. That's every year that happens [...] every year, every school I've ever worked in, I've managed to end up with a piece of artwork and I've got them framed on my wall. And I still look at them and I can still remember like [names of pupils] and just seeing them smile. The recognition that you're there for them. That's always been incredibly precious. (Dan, secondary school teacher)*

A commitment to improving students' lives was a strong motivator for many participants. Primary school teacher Gail commented, 'I enjoy coming into school and seeing the children; I enjoy teaching; I enjoy making a difference; I enjoy the special needs and meeting parents'. Secondary teacher Henry remembered why he had become a teacher in the first place, commenting, 'it was about the kids, and giving them the opportunities that they deserved'.

Secondary school teacher Cathy explained that her generation had been 'idealists' and that her aspiration had always been 'to work with kids in communities that were struggling, and enable them to have a good time'. This aspiration continued to motivate her 40 years on:

> *The most wonderful thing is, when you see and experience kids grappling with chaotic home lives, and yet they are actually getting a sense of who they are and achieving as individuals and feeling*

*good about themselves [...] I mean, I don't think there's anything
greater than that. (Cathy, secondary school teacher)*

Her commitment to social justice had underpinned Cathy's motivation to
take on the types of roles she had undertaken. For example, she talked about
her involvement in the 'extended school' initiative, which was,

> *about disadvantaged learners of all abilities [...] It talks about
> failing schools, but people recognized that there were failing
> communities, and so the extended school was about putting in
> place social workers in schools, school nurses and other supportive
> individuals [...] If you got that right, the idea was that [children]
> had a better chance of meeting their potential in the classroom.
> (Cathy, secondary school teacher)*

Cathy described the school in which she was working at the time of the
interview as,

> *a very turbulent school, with a big white British council estate
> intake [and] also a massive number of English as Additional
> Language students, who can't speak English. Because we've always
> had places in this school, it means that anyone coming in to the
> country, into [city], have come here, so, in any one year we could
> have as many as, oh, a hundred and eighty young people coming,
> on top of the kids we've already got. So, in any one week, teachers
> would have to take on say, fifteen new youngsters from little Indian
> villages, where they've never seen a computer [...] [So we have]
> a big EAL population, who have had no schooling in their own
> country. When they come here, not only have they not got English
> but they're not used to learning. So really, I'm now working with
> groups of students [...] to make sure we do our best for them and
> that they achieve what they can. (Cathy, secondary school teacher)*

The teachers' continued dedication to making a difference, engendering
success and putting children first had endured. This is perhaps surprising,
given their descriptions of an educational culture fixated on results, and a profession characterised by high workload, high levels of stress and long working hours. In this connection, participants talked about the need to ensure
a healthy work–life balance for themselves and others. Their awareness of
the need to do this seemed to be a factor that helped them to cope with the
demands of the job, even if they were in general not satisfied with the balance
they had achieved, as I show in the next section.

TEACHERS' CONCERN TO MAINTAIN
A WORK–LIFE BALANCE

It was apparent that even very experienced teachers have to work long hours to meet the many demands of their job. Workload, an unsatisfactory work–life balance, stress and anxiety all featured in the teachers' accounts of their daily work. Some had developed strategies to help them more or less cope, which often included drawing on the support of others. In general, being mindful of the need to try to balance work and home or private life seemed to help some teachers to gain a sense of perspective on what was important, and what to prioritise. The scope and ability to prioritise helped them to sustain their commitment to teaching.

In this section, I draw on two narratives to provide examples of the types of responses we gathered relating to managing work–life balance. The first is from Gail, who reported that she loved her job but that it was being spoiled by an unreasonable, unmanageable and unsustainable workload that resulted mainly from Ofsted categorising her school as 'requires improvement'. The second is from Barbara, who felt that teachers needed to develop resilience and take charge of their own pace of work in order to cope.

> At the moment, it is just too much work. I do work stupid hours just to plan lessons and to get through stuff. We have to do triple marking. We can't stop it until Ofsted have been and gone [...] So, at the moment I just feel very tired. I enjoy my job, but I'm very tired. The workload is outrageous. The teachers' workload is completely outrageous. There are so many young teachers giving up, and that has happened here, when they never finish their NQT year or they have a breakdown [...] We've got quite a few young ones who just want to stay as TAs, who are very competent. For most of us our work–life balance is absolutely rubbish [...] The accountability and the requirements to do all this marking – even though the government says that we don't have to do all this marking in actual fact – nobody dares stop any of the stuff that we are doing; nobody is brave enough to do that unless they are in an outstanding school. Because we are vulnerable, we are made to work to the nth degree [...] Some of our children are of a very low standard when they come in. We work very hard, but we've got some very disturbed and vulnerable children here who are sometimes quite tricky to manage. And you are managing that, and quite a high level of special needs, and trying to get them all to make progress. So, I think workload is almost untenable for all of us. (Gail, primary school teacher)

Reflecting on how she had stayed the course for over 40 years, primary school teacher Barbara commented:

You just have to be resilient, because there are a lot of down times.
There are a lot of new things you think you're never going to crack.
I do think I am a bit of a plodder. And I think you have to plod,
and I think that's the way I've got through really. I think if you are
too particular and you take it too much to heart, you will never
last. And to me it's always been a job. I've always had my home. My
life outside. And it's been a job, not particularly the be all and end
all of my life. And I think that's another secret to it really. (Barbara,
primary school teacher)

The two positions expressed above are illustrative of the range of perspectives expressed across the sample. Workload was unquestionably an issue for all participants, consistent with the body of literature on workload and accountability, cited in Chapter 2 (e.g. Berryhill et al., 2009; Day & Smethem, 2009; Valli & Buese, 2007; Wood, 2019). The teachers' responses to their heavy workloads included working longer hours for at least periods of time to meet externally imposed demands, as Gail explained, and elements of taking control, deciding what to spend more time on, as in Barbara's case. The scope to take control and ownership appears to have been a factor enabling teachers to remain in the profession during an era of much policy change.

Although the teachers had seen an unwelcome rise in workload, they had, to a greater or lesser extent, managed to maintain some work–life balance. On the one hand, they identified the anxiety and heavy workloads involved in teaching, describing periods when there was little, if any, work–life balance. On the other hand, they talked about understanding the negative impacts that heavy workloads can have, and how they attempted to develop more sustainable approaches to their work. These approaches included developing individual resilience, but also focusing on life beyond school so that teaching did not become an all-consuming lifestyle.

The changing policy environment – embodied in the National Curriculum and associated assessment regimes, heightened accountability, and Ofsted – was perceived by the teachers to have had a generally negative impact on school cultures over time. Yet, whilst the national picture was seen as predominantly negative, the perceptions from participants about their own work, and how they made it enjoyable and sustainable, reflect a strong sense of agency and vocation. They re-claimed their freedom and autonomy in the classroom, and they took steps to manage their workload. By working collaboratively and building positive relationships, many of the participants believed they could create professional spaces, which policies had tended to restrict. Committed to an ethic of care for young people, the teachers also had a continued joy of working with children, particularly in helping those from less wealthy backgrounds gain a more equal set of life opportunities. It was by focusing on these factors that many of the participants believed they had been able to have positive impacts, albeit at a personal or local level. Their belief in their own capacity to make a difference reinforced their sense of professional freedom. Their certainty that there was still the potential to make a positive difference fuelled their motivation and sense of vocation. A belief in their capacity to have positive impact was central, it would seem, to their longevity.

In Chapter 8, I revisit the methodological approach taken in this study, considering the scope it offers for generating rich data and deep understandings of teachers' perceptions and experiences. I acknowledge the limitations of the study. I summarise the new insights gleaned in this investigation, and present a conceptual model in the form of an 'ideal type' that captures the characteristics of the career-long teacher, helping us to understand why they stay in the profession.

NOTE

1. Continuing professional development.

Chapter 8

UNDERSTANDING THE LIVED
EXPERIENCE AND LONGEVITY
OF THE CAREER-LONG TEACHER

INTRODUCTION

The interviews undertaken in this study were original in that they focussed on career-long teachers' lived experiences and perceptions of implementing government-imposed change over a 30-year period, in the context of English state education. The study used a novel methodology to investigate the teachers' career-long experiences, and in the first part of this chapter, I consider the affordances of the approach taken. Drawing on the data generated from the nine narratives, I then present a conceptual model of an ideal type of career-long teacher, in order to capture the original insights offered by the study.

AFFORDANCES OF THE RESEARCH DESIGN

The research design combined a semi-structured interview with a retrospective, narrative approach, so harnessing a longitudinal view. The participants were asked to reflect back over time, so the study has some features of life history interviews, applied to career-long experiences of policy change implementation. The interview was based on a checklist of core areas to discuss, rather than fixed questions. The questioning was deliberately open-ended so that the participants would be able to define for themselves what the critical points of their experience had been, for example, recalling the policies that had the greatest impact on their work. Interviewers did not 'suggest' particular policies to consider, but allowed participants to set the agenda for the discussion by sharing their thoughts and recollections. This open-ended approach provides authentic narratives with meaning for the narrators, and allows the interviewer scope for probing to elicit richer, more detailed accounts.

Our analytical strategy was based on the principles of IPA, following the guidance of psychologists Smith et al. (2009). IPA studies are still relatively unusual in educational research, being primarily based on idiographic rather than generic experiences, although there are some examples (such as Guihen, 2020; Noon, 2018; Smith, 2017; Woodhouse & Pedder, 2016). IPA is suitable for articulate participants, such as our teachers, whose descriptions and reflections were full, detailed, insightful and often analytical. On reflection, there is considerable scope, when using this approach with a small number of participants, to include in the report more detailed accounts of the individual stories. In this book, a balance was struck between relating individuals' experiences and ascertaining where there was commonality, in order to identify the most common themes to emerge from the study.

The data provided new insights into the sophisticated processes whereby the career-long teachers take ownership of change to suit the contexts within which they work, and the students they teach. Participants' perspectives offered complex and nuanced understandings of the nature of their daily work post-1988. Their accounts provided a view of teaching that contrasted with that portrayed in the teachers' standards, where teacher professionalism is defined simply in terms of a set of desired behaviours (see Evans, 2011). The competency statements in the standards take little account of values, vocation or expertise developed over time. Yet this study has shown that the decisions the career-long teachers make are grounded in experience, their commitment to making a positive difference to children's lives, and a set of values that fuel their motivation to persevere in their chosen vocation. Their narratives provide a rounded view of a long-term career founded on an ethic of care, positive working relationships and a grounded sense of self-belief.

UNDERSTANDING THE LONGEVITY OF THE CAREER-LONG TEACHER: NEW INSIGHTS

Drawing on the data from all nine narratives, I present below a conceptual model in the form of an 'ideal type' of the career long-teacher in post-1988 England (see Fig. 1). Whilst the model draws on findings from all of the participants, as an ideal type, it is not intended to be an exact match for any one person.

The model suggests that a combination of vocation and wisdom empowers teachers to exert their agency in taking ownership of required change, and in developing strategies for contextualised policy implementation. In this model, vocation comprises values and motivation; wisdom comprises vision, expertise and control; and agency comprises ownership and strategy. Fig. 1 provides further details, drawing on the data from this study to identify the factors that make up each element of the three constituent parts of the model.

The first constituent in the ideal type model is 'vocation', in which I bring together the core values the teacher espouses, and their principal sources of motivation. Essentially, the teacher loves teaching. They love what they teach, and they enjoy working with young people. Children are their first priority. Any change the teacher is required to make in their classroom practices in response to policy imperatives must be made to work to the benefit of the children in their care. The teacher enjoys autonomy, and the freedom to make their own decisions in the classroom. They are committed to making a difference to children's lives and enabling them to flourish. This commitment has remained constant career-long, fuelling their motivation and giving meaning to their work. They derive the greatest satisfaction from seeing students enjoy their learning and achieve their potential, and their work is underpinned by a commitment to social justice. Appreciation from pupils motivates and sustains them, reminding them of why they entered the teaching profession in the first place.

The teacher is committed to teamwork and collegiality. They derive satisfaction from working collaboratively, and they contribute, through their work with others, to maintaining a culture of collaboration and teamwork in their schools. They identify positively with their schools, where they feel a sense of belonging. Positive working relationships are very important to them, and their relationships with children and colleagues are based on an ethic of care and empathy. The ethic of care also extends to self-care, in that they are very aware of the need to try to achieve a work–life balance. They have developed some strategies to enable this to be possible.

The second constituent in the model is 'wisdom'. Wisdom is defined as 'accumulated knowledge', and, 'the ability to think and act utilising knowledge, experience, understanding, common sense and insight' (*Collins English Dictionary and Thesaurus*, 2002). In the model, I differentiate three elements that constitute wisdom: vision, expertise and control.

Within the 'vision' element is the ability to envisage the scope for positive change. This is arguably one of the most important factors in the model. Without this ability, it would seem unlikely that the teacher would maintain the commitment and motivation to sustain them long term. Added to this is the teacher's clarity about the primary purpose of their role, which they see in terms of offering opportunities to children. Finally, they believe firmly in their

VOCATION comprising Values and Motivating Factors for Policy Implementation

Values	Motivating factors
Children first priority	Ensuring change works to benefit of children
Commitment to student success	Satisfaction derived from student success
Commitment to making a difference to students' lives	Love of teaching
Commitment to social justice	Love of subject
Ethic of care and empathy towards children and colleagues	Pupils' enjoyment of lessons
Ethic of care extended to self: need for life-work balance	Freedom and autonomy in classroom
Positive working relationships important	Liking for young people
Commitment to team work and collegiality	Enjoyment of collaboration with colleagues
Emotional engagement with school	Sense of belonging & personal identification with school

WISDOM comprising Vision, Expertise and Control

Vision	Expertise	Control
Ability to see how change can be positive	Confidence, grounded in sustained experience and expertise	Belief that they can take control of change
Sees role as providing opportunities for children	See themselves as able to improve students' lives	Ability to prioritise
Belief in the scope to exert a positive impact	Self-belief	Belief in own freedom and capacity to act

AGENCY, comprising Ownership and Strategy

Ownership	Strategy for policy implementation
Acts autonomously	Takes time to interpret policy
Takes ownership of change	Mediates policy
Draws on available sources of support	Tailors policy to children & school context
Takes control of pace of change	Implements change at a manageable pace

Fig. 1. Conceptual Model of the Career-long Teacher: An Ideal Type.

own capacity to exert a positive impact and to make positive change happen in their teaching role.

The second element of wisdom is 'expertise'. The career-long teacher has a strong sense of self-belief, and confidence in their own knowledge and skill, grounded in their sustained experience of teaching. They have a clear view of themselves as able to improve students' lives.

The third element is control, that is, a belief that they can take control of change in their own classrooms and schools. They are able to prioritise the areas they will aim to change, and how. Decisions about what to prioritise are informed by their values, and how they do it is informed by their experience. A fundamental belief in their own freedom and capacity to act underpins their willingness and determination to take control and ownership of change, and the pace of change.

Vocation and wisdom combine to foster teacher agency, the third constituent part of the model. As Fig. 1 shows, agency includes taking ownership of, and developing strategy for, policy implementation. The teacher is also agentic in drawing on a range of sources of support to sustain them in taking ownership of change in their schools and classrooms. Their working lives are strengthened and supported by reciprocal, supportive, familial relationships in schools. Collaborations with colleagues motivate and energise them, and strengthen their sense of belonging in the school, to which they feel a positive, emotional attachment. Their school 'family', empowering senior leaders and positive, supportive home lives are all important sources of support, on which they draw proactively.

The teacher's belief in their own agency and scope to manage change leads them to take the time to reflect on policy before implementation. The teacher acts autonomously in the choices and judgements they make in their daily work. They unpick, analyse and adjust policy as they translate it into practice, so that it is fit for purpose. They engage in a process of interpretation and mediation of policy, before tailoring the changes to suit the children they teach and the context in which they are teaching, at a pace that is manageable. They are neither resistant to nor compliant with government imperatives, but make pragmatic judgements about the extent to which they can tailor change to suit their students, classrooms and schools. They evaluate the degree of freedom that they have to make their own decisions about pedagogy and curriculum content, and they take ownership of change. They take policy, and make it work, for their students and their school.

It is noteworthy that the model works at optimal level when all components are fully functioning and working together. Were any part to be missing or dysfunctional, the operation breaks down. For example, in a school in which the collaborative culture or commitment to teamwork are weak, or the senior leadership unsupportive, even the most committed career-long teacher may eventually disengage. Similarly, should the teacher lose faith in their own capacity to exert positive change, demoralisation and disengagement would be likely to ensue. It may be that, in this sense, the model accounts not only for why teachers remain career-long, but also why they quit. This might provide the basis for further research, as the findings of the current study point to remarkably committed teachers who stay the course despite the challenge of constant change.

CONCLUDING COMMENTS

This book reports on experienced teachers' perceptions of and reflections on an extraordinary period of educational history in England, 1988–2018. This was an era characterised by a succession of reforms that changed the culture of schooling and the work of teachers. The book provides authentic and original insights into the impact of reform on teachers' daily work, drawing on the career experiences of nine teachers near the end of their careers, who had lived through and implemented the changes. More significantly, it offers new understandings of why these teachers stayed the course, given the shifting policy context.

Over time many of the participants in this study had gained in confidence. Linked to their confidence was their ability to focus on the positive and exert their professional agency. This confidence had allowed them to be increasingly selective in what they adopted in their practice, rather than following change, both national and organisational, uncritically and in fine detail. They were able to look beyond the constraints and see the scope for positive change, a key factor that helped to sustain and retain the rich seam of teaching expertise afforded by this generation of career-long teachers.

The findings of this study might usefully inform policymakers and school leaders concerned to retain teachers in the profession. The insights gained might also be of interest to novice teachers, or those considering the profession, as they reflect on their motivation and potential strategies for dealing with far-reaching policy shifts that are likely to impact their work during the course of their careers. For the teachers in this study, their core values, wisdom, sense of vocation and firm belief in the scope and the imperative to make a positive difference to children's lives emerged as highly important in securing their long-term commitment to the teaching profession.

REFERENCES

Ainsworth, S., & Oldfield, J. (2019). Quantifying teacher resilience: Context matters. *Teaching and Teacher Education*, 82, 117–128. doi:10.1016/j.tate.2019.03.012

Anilkumar, A. (2023, January 10). 2023 Ofsted ratings and reports explained for parents and teachers [Blog] Third Space Learning. Retrieved from https://thirdspacelearning.com/blog/ofsted-ratings-reports/

Ball, S. (2003). The teacher's soul and the terrors of performativity. *Journal of Education Policy*, 18(2), 215–228. doi:10.1080/0268093022000043065

Baxter, J. A. (2013). Professional inspector or inspecting professional? Teachers as inspectors in a new regulatory regime for education in England. *Cambridge Journal of Education*, 43(4), 467–485. doi:10.1080/030576 4X.2013.819069

Baxter, J., Grek, S., & Segerholm, C. (2015). Regulatory frameworks: Shifting frameworks, shifting criteria. In S. Grek & J. Lindgren (Eds.), *Governing by inspection* (pp. 74–96). London: Routledge.

Berryhill, J., Linney, J. A., & Fromewick, J. (2009). The effects of education accountability on teachers: Are policies too stress provoking for their own good? *International Journal of Education Policy and Leadership*, 4(5), 1–14. doi:10.22230/ijepl.2009v4n5a99

Biesta, G. (2009). Good education in an age of measurement: On the need to reconnect with the question of purpose in education. *Education Assessment Evaluation and Accountability*, 21, 33–46. doi:10.1007/s11092-008-9064-9

Boldrini, E., Sappa, V., & Aprea, C. (2019). Which difficulties and resources do vocational teachers perceive? An exploratory study setting the stage for investigating teachers' resilience in Switzerland. *Teachers and Teaching*, 25(1), 125–141. doi:10.1080/13540602.2018.1520086

Brighouse, T., & Waters, M. (2022). *About our schools: Improving on previous best*. Camarthen: Crown House Publishing.

Callaghan, J. (1976, October 18). A rational debate based on the facts [Speech] Ruskin College, Oxford. Education in England: The History of Our Schools. Retrieved from https://education-uk.org/documents/speeches/1976ruskin.html

Chiong, C., Menzies, L., & Parameshwaran, M. (2017). Why do long-serving teachers stay in the teaching profession? Analysing the motivations of teachers with 10 or more years' experience in England. *British Educational Research Journal*, *43*(6), 1083–1110. doi:10.1002/berj.3302

Collins English dictionary and thesaurus. (2000). (2nd ed.). Glasgow: HarperCollins.

Connell, L. A., McMahon, N. E., & Adams, N. (2014). Stroke survivors' experiences of somatosensory impairment after stroke: An interpretative phenomenological analysis. *Physiotherapy*, *100*(2), 150–155. doi:10.1016/j.physio.2013.09.003

Craft, A., & Jeffrey, B. (2008). *Creativity and performativity in teaching and learning (CAPITAL) Version 2: Full research report*. ESRC End of Award Report RES-000-23-1281, ESRC, Swindon.

Day, C. (2004). *A passion for teaching*. London: Routledge Falmer.

Day, C. (2008). Committed for life? Variations in teachers' work, lives and effectiveness. *Journal of Educational Change*, *9*(3), 243–260. doi:10.1007/s10833-007-9054-6

Day, C., & Gu, Q. (2014). *Resilient teachers, resilient schools: Building and sustaining quality in testing times*. London: Routledge.

Day, C., & Hong, J. (2016). Influences on the capacities for emotional resilience of teachers in schools serving disadvantaged urban communities: Challenges of living on the edge. *Teaching and Teacher Education*, *59*, 115–125. doi:10.1016/j.tate.2016.05.015

Day, C., Sammons, P., Hopkins, D., Harris, A., Leithwood, K., Gu, Q., Penlington, C., Mehta, P., & Kington, A. (2007). The impact of school leadership on pupil outcomes: Interim Report No DCSF-RR018. Nottingham: DCSF Publications.

Day, C., & Smethem, L. (2009). The effects of reform: Have teachers really lost their sense of professionalism? *Journal of Educational Change*, *10*(2–3), 141–157.

Denscombe, M. (2010). *The good research guide for small-scale social research projects* (4th ed.). Maidenhead: Open University Press.

Department for Education (DfE). (2011). *The national strategies 1997–2011*. Retrieved from https://www.gov.uk/government/publications/the-national-strategies-1997-to-2011

Department for Education (DfE). (2017). *School workforce in England: November 2018*. Retrieved from https://www.gov.uk/government/statistics/school-workforce-in-england-november-2018

Dumay, X., & Galand, B. (2011). The multilevel impact of transformational leadership on teacher commitment: Cognitive and motivational pathways. *British Educational Research Journal, 38*(5), 703–729. doi:10.1080/01411926.2011.577889

Dunn, W. (2019, March 4). Ten years on, schools are still fighting academisation. *The New Statesman*. Retrieved from https://www.newstatesman.com/spotlight/2019/03/ten-years-schools-are-still-fighting-academisation

Ehren, M., & Baxter, J. (2021). Governance of education systems: Trust, accountability and capacity in hierarchies, markets and networks. In M. Ehren & J. Baxter (Eds.), *Trust, accountability and capacity in education system reform: Global perspectives in comparative education* (pp. 30–54). London: Routledge.

Evans, L. (2011). The 'shape' of teacher professionalism in England: professional standards, performance management, professional development and the changes proposed in the 2010 White Paper. *British Educational Research Journal, 37*(5), 851–870.

Fan, W., & Liang, Y. (2020). The impact of school autonomy and education marketization in the United Kingdom. *Journal of Policy Modeling, 42*, 1038–1048. doi:10.1016/j.jpolmod.2020.04.007

Fernet, C., Guay, F., Senécal, C., & Austin, S. (2012). Predicting individual changes in teacher burnout: The role of perceived school environment and motivational factors. *Teaching and Teacher Education, 28*, 514–525. doi:10.1016/j.tate.2011.11.013

Fielding, M. (2006). Leadership, personalization and high performance schooling: Naming the new totalitarianism. *School Leadership and Management, 26*(4), 347–369. doi:10.1080/13632430600886889

Fisher, T. (2008). The era of centralisation: The 1988 Education Reform Act and its consequences. *Forum, 50*(2), 255–261. doi:10.2304/forum.2008.50.2.255

George, C. (2009). *The psychological contract*. Maidenhead: Open University Press.

Gillard, D. (2018). Education in England: A history – Timeline. Retrieved from http://educationengland.org.uk/history

Gilligan, C. (1982). *In a different voice*. Cambridge, MA: Harvard University Press.

Glazer, J. (2018). Leaving lessons: Learning from the exit decisions of experienced teachers. *Teachers and Teaching, 24*(1), 50–62. doi:10.1080/13540602.2017.1383238

Greaney, T. (2015, September 9). How are academies, academy chains, and the "self-improving school system" developing in England? A podcast with Toby Greaney. *International Education News*. Retrieved from https://internationalednews.com/2015/09/09/how-are-academies-academy-chains-and-the-self-improving-school-system-developing-in-england-a-podcast-with-toby-greany/

Green, J. (2011). *Education, professionalism and the quest for accountability: Hitting the target but missing the point*. Abingdon: Routledge.

Gu, Q. (2014). The role of relational resilience in teachers' career long commitment and effectiveness. *Teachers and Teaching, 20*(5), 505–529. doi:10.1080/13540602.2014.937961

Gu, Q., & Day, C. (2013). Challenges to teacher resilience: Conditions count. *British Educational Research Journal, 39*(1), 22–44. doi:10.1080/01411926.2011.623152

Guihen, L. (2020). Using interpretative phenomenological analysis (IPA) to explore the career experiences of women deputy headteachers. *International Journal of Research & Method in Education, 43*(5), 526–540. doi:10.1080/1743727X.2019.1693537

Hallahan, G. (2023, May 5). Where did all the over-50s teachers go? *TES Magazine*. Retrieved from https://www.tes.com/magazine/analysis/general/teacher-retention-decline-over-50

Han, J., & Yin, H. (2016). Teacher motivation: Definition, research development and implications for teachers. *Cogent Education, 3*(1), 1–18. doi:10.1080/2331186X.2016.1217819

Hobbs, L. (2012). Examining the aesthetic dimensions of teaching: Relationships between teacher knowledge, identity and passion.

Teaching and Teacher Education, 28(5), 718–727. doi:10.1016/j.tate.2012.01.010

Ingersoll, R. M., & Smith, T. M. (2003). The wrong solution to the teacher shortage. *Educational Leadership, 60*, 30–33. doi:10.4236/oalib.1101404

Kanter, R. M. (1983). *The change masters: Innovation and entrepreneurship in the American corporation.* New York, NY: Simon and Schuster.

Kyriacou, C., & Coulthard, M. (2000). Undergraduates' views of teaching as a career choice. *Journal of Education for Teaching, 26*(2), 117–126. doi:10.1080/02607470050127036

Labaree, D. F. (2011). Targeting teachers. *Dissent*, Summer, 9–14. doi:10.1353/dss.2011.0068

Lee, J., & Fitz, J. (1997). HMI and Ofsted: Evolution or revolution in school inspection. *British Journal of Educational Studies, 45*(1), 39–52.

Lingard, B., Martino, W., & Rezai-Rashti, G. (2013). Testing regimes, accountabilities and education policy: Commensurate global and national developments. *Journal of Education Policy, 28*(5), 539–556. doi:10.1080/02680939.2013.820042

Mancuso, S. V., Roberts, L., & White, G. P. (2011). Teacher retention in international schools: The key role of school leadership. *Journal of Research in International Education, 9*(3), 306–323. doi:10.1177/1475240910388928

Mason, J. (2018). *Qualitative researching* (3rd ed.). London: Sage.

McGuire, J. M. (2022). Margaret Thatcher's UK school reforms – Aims, impact, and legacy. *Social and Education History, 11*(3), 228–244. doi:10.17583/hse.10645

McIntyre, J. (2010). Why they sat still: The ideas and values of long-serving teachers in challenging, inner-city schools in England. *Teachers and Teaching: Theory and Practice, 16*(5), 595–614. doi:10.1080/13540602.2010.507968

Morgan, W., & Wells, M. (2016). 'It's deemed unmanly': men's experiences of intimate partner violence (IPV). *The Journal of Forensic Psychiatry & Psychology, 27*(3), 404–418. https://doi.org/10.1080/14789949.2015.1127986

Noon, E. J. (2018). Interpretative phenomenological analysis: An appropriate methodology for educational research? *Journal of Perspectives in Applied Academic Practice, 6*(1), 75–83. doi:10.14297/jpaap.v6i1.304

Ovenden-Hope, T., Blandford, S., Cain, T., & Maxwell, B. (2018). RETAIN early career teacher retention programme: Evaluating the role of research informed continuing professional development for a high quality, sustainable 21st century teaching profession. *Journal of Education for Teaching, 44*(5), 590–607. doi:10.1080/02607476.2018.1516349

Ozga, J. (1995). Deskilling a profession: Professionalism, deprofessionalisation and the new managerialism. In H. Busher & R. Saran (Eds.), *Managing teachers as professionals in schools* (pp. 21–37). London: Kogan Page.

Ozga, J., Baxter, J., Clarke, J., Grek, S., & Lawn, M. (2013). The politics of educational change: Governance and school inspection in England and Scotland. *Swiss Journal of Sociology, 39*(2), 37–55.

Perrachione, B. A., Rosser, V. J., & Petersen, G. J. (2008). Why do they stay? Elementary teachers' perceptions of job satisfaction and retention. *Professional Educator, 32*(2), 1–17.

Reid, J. (2018). *Primary teachers, inspection and the silencing of the ethic of care.* Bingley: Emerald Publishing.

Ryan, S. V., von der Embse, N. P., Pendergast, L. L., Saeki, E., Segool, N., & Schwing, S. (2017). Leaving the teaching profession: The role of teacher stress and educational accountability policies on turnover intent. *Teaching and Teacher Education, 66*, 1–11. doi:10.1016/j.tate.2017.03.016

Sahlberg, P. (2012). *Finnish lessons: What can the world learn from educational change in Finland?* New York, NY: Teachers' College Press.

Schmidt, M., & Datnow, A. (2005). Teachers' sense-making about comprehensive school reform: The influence of emotions. *Teaching and Teacher Education, 21*, 949–965. doi:10.1016/j.tate.2005.06.006

Shah, M., & Abualrob, M. M. A. (2012). Teacher collegiality and teacher professional commitment in public secondary schools in Islamabad, Pakistan. *Procedia Social and Behavioral Sciences, 46*, 950–954. doi:10.1016/j.sbspro.2012.05.229

Shinebourne, P., & Smith, J. A. (2010). 'It is just habitual': An interpretative phenomenological analysis of the experience of long-term recovery from addiction. *International Journal of Mental Health and Addiction, 9*(3), 282–295. doi:10.1007/s11469-010-9286-1

Six, F. (2021). Trust-based accountability in education: The role of intrinsic motivation. In M. Ehren & J. Baxter (Eds.), *Trust, accountability and capacity in education system reform: Global perspectives in comparative education* (pp. 55–77). London: Routledge.

Skaalvik, E. M., & Skaalvik, S. (2017). Motivated for teaching? Associations with school goal structure, teacher self efficacy, job satisfaction and emotional exhaustion. *Teaching and Teacher Education, 67*, 152–160. doi:10.1016/j.tate.2017.06.006

Smith, A. R. T. (2017). Insights into shifting perspectives of the Gypsy and Traveller community on schooling, and implications for leaders. *Management in Education, 31*(1), 14–20. doi:10.1177/08920206

Smith, J. (2008). Maslow, motivation and female teachers' career decisions. *Psychology of Women Section Review, 10*(1), 22–30.

Smith, J. (2012). Reflections on using life history to investigate women teachers' aspirations and career decisions. *Qualitative Research, 12*(4), 486–503.

Smith, J. A., Flowers, P., & Larkin, M. (2009). *Interpretative phenomenological analysis: Theory, method and research.* London: Sage.

Stevenson, H., & Wood, P. (2013). Markets, managerialism and teachers' work: The invisible hand of high stakes testing in England. *The International Education Journal: Comparative Perspectives, 12*(1), 42–61.

Stigler, J. W., & Hiebert, J. (1999). *The teaching gap: Best ideas from the world's teachers for improving in the classroom.* New York, NY: The Free Press.

Sugrue, C. (2006). A critical appraisal of the impact of international agencies on educational reforms and teachers' lives and work: The case of Ireland? *European Educational Research Journal, 5*(3), 181–195. doi:10.2304/eerj.2006.5.3.181

Szczesiul, S., & Huizenga, J. (2014). The burden of leadership: Exploring the principal's role in teacher collaboration. *Improving Schools, 17*(2), 176–191. doi:10.1177/1365480214534545

Thomas, G. (2009). *How to do your research project.* London: Sage.

Troman, G. (2007). *Primary teacher identity, commitment and career in performative cultures: Full research report.* ESRC End of Award Report RES-00-23-0748, ESRC, Swindon.

Valli, L., & Buese, D. (2007). The changing roles of teachers in an era of high-stakes accountability. *American Educational Research Association, 44*(3), 519–558. doi:10.3102/0002831207306859

Watson, G. (2001). The national curriculum. In S. Capel, M. Leask, & T. Turner (Eds.), *Learning to teach in the secondary school* (3rd ed., pp. 347–361). London: Routledge Falmer.

Weiss, E. M. (1999). Perceived workplace conditions and first year teachers' morale, career choice commitment, and planned retention: A secondary analysis. *Teaching and Teacher Education, 15*(8), 861–879. doi:10.1016/S0742-051X(99)00040-2

West, A., & Bailey, E. (2013). "The development of the academies programme: 'Privatising' school-based education in England 1986–2013. *British Journal of Educational Studies, 61*(2), 137–159. doi:10.1080/00071005.2013.789480

Whitty, G. (2008). Twenty years of progress? English education policy 1988 to the present. *Educational Management Administration and Leadership, 36*(2), 165–184. doi:10.1177/174114320708771

Wood, P. (2019). Rethinking time in the workload debate. *Management in Education, 33*(2), 86–90. doi:10.1177/0892020618823481

Wood, P., & Smith, J. (2016). *Educational research: Taking the plunge.* Camarthen: Independent Thinking Press.

Woodhouse, J., & Pedder, D. (2016). Early career teachers' perceptions and experiences of leadership development: balancing structure and agency in contrasting school contexts. *Research Papers in Education, 32*(5), 553–577. doi:10.1080/02671522.2016.1225794

Woods, P., & Simkins, T. (2014). Understanding the local: Themes and issues in the experience of structural reform in England. *Educational Management Administration & Leadership, 42*(3), 324–340. doi:10.1177/1741143214521587

ABOUT THE AUTHOR

Joan Woodhouse has been teaching for over 40 years. Following her early career experience as a teacher of English as a Second Language, she taught secondary modern foreign languages for approximately 18 years, mainly in large, urban comprehensive schools in the English Midlands. During that time, she was appointed to a range of middle and senior secondary school leadership posts, moving into Higher Education in 2001. Initially appointed to a post as Senior Lecturer in Secondary Education at Canterbury Christ Church University, she later took up a position at the University of Leicester, where she is currently Associate Professor of Education. She has a keen research interest in teachers' lives and careers. Her PhD thesis focussed on life histories and career decisions of women teachers and headteachers. More recently, she has investigated the aspirations and experiences of student teachers, early career teachers, career-long teachers and student teachers who are mothers. She lives in Leicestershire and is happily married to John, a mechanical engineer, her best friend and anchor.

INDEX

Printed and bound by CPI Group (UK) Ltd, Croydon, CR0 4YY

11/12/2023

08206190-0001